W9-CXO-784

Accounting Fundamentals for Nonfinancial Managers

(Revised Edition)

by Allen Sweeny

A DIVISION OF AMERICAN MANAGEMENT ASSOCIATIONS

Allen Sweeny is controller-treasurer of the International Division of Standard Brands Incorporated. This collection, a series of articles reprinted from Supervisory Management, is a revision and condensation of the author's AMACOM book, Accounting Fundamentals for Nonfinancial Executives. The condensation was edited by Thomasine Rendero.

Contents

Part 1: The basic concepts

An understanding of the basic concepts of accounting and finance is critical to the successful performance of every manager, whether he likes it or not. This series presents those concepts in a simple, straightforward manner. Although it won't train any accountants, it can help the busy nonfinancial manager become knowledgeable about (1) fundamental accounting and financial concepts and practices, and (2) the uses, as well as the limitations, of those practices in the managerial process.

To do this, we shall place more emphasis on concepts and essentials and less on explanations of debits, credits, and ledgers, since our purpose is to explain how to use, rather than how to create, financial data. More important, we shall concentrate on the inherently commonsensical aspects of the accounting and financial function. The basic concepts underlying the accounting function are the keys to understanding it and are often amazingly simple—however complex the function may become in a large, complex organization.

To explore these propositions more specifically, let's begin with the two concepts at the heart of all accounting theory and practice: first the dual aspect principle and then the accrual concept.

THE DUAL ASPECT PRINCIPLE

Let's illustrate the dual aspect with a hypothetical but common personal situation, the purchase of a home. This activity involves screening and selecting the house to be bought, and then arranging the necessary financing. Assume that the house can be purchased for $40,000 and that to make this purchase, we wish to borrow $30,000, to be financed through a conventional 25-year mortgage loan.

Next, we must convince some friendly banker of our credit worthiness. To evaluate our credit standing, he will want to know whether we can make the necessary down payment on the house and then repay the mortgage loan with interest over the next 25 years.

Specifically, he will want to know what things of value we own and how much money we owe and to whom. Assume that our response to these questions looks like this:

Things of Value		Amount Owed	
Cash		Personal bank loan	$2,000
Checking account	$ 500		
Savings	5,500		
Stock at current			
market value	8,000		
Total	$14,000		

For the sake of brevity, assume that our personal financial situation meets with approval, and that we (along with our friendly banker) now become happy homeowners. As a result of this transaction, our financial situation now looks like this:

Things of Value		Amounts Owed	
Cash		Personal bank loan	$ 2,000
Checking account	$ 500	25-year mortgage loan	30,000
Stock	3,500	Total	$32,000
House	40,000		
Total	$44,000		

Through this simple and familiar process, we have not only be-come homeowners but have also made use of some key accounting concepts. For example, one of the basic facts in which our banker was interested was what things of value we owned. The same ques-tion could be phrased: What are your assets? *Assets* is the word accountants use to describe things of value measurable in monetary terms. We were asked to list our assets in our bank application.

We were also asked to list what we owed and to whom. Such obli-gations, referred to as "liabilities," represent a legal commitment. To be legally obligated is, in fact, to be liable. Another way to think of liabilities is as a claim on our assets. The person to whom we are liable has a claim on our assets up to the amount of credit he had extended to us. Another word for a claim such as this is "equity." Special courts, called "courts of equity," specialize in the just and impartial settlement of contending claims. In our particular illustra-tion, our creditor (the bank) extended to us a personal loan of $2,000, and we were liable to him for a claim on assets in this amount. In this case and all others, the claim of the creditor on these assets is a liability.

If this liability is $2,000, there are obviously still $12,000 of assets to be claimed, and the next logical question is: Who has a claim on these? If no other creditors have a claim on these assets, obviously we, the owner, have a claim on them; they are called "owner's equity." Thus there can be two types of equities (claims against our assets)—liabilities, or claims of lenders or creditors, and owner's equity, or claims of the owners.

In terms of assets, liabilities, and equities, the financial information on the loan application before and after purchase would appear as shown at the top of the opposite page.

We can see by comparing these tables that although we now own a home, our personal, or owner's, equity remains unchanged after the purchase. Why? Because although our assets increased, a cor-responding increase occurred in the creditor's claim on those assets.

Assets, Liabilities, and Equities

BEFORE PURCHASE

Assets		Equities	
Cash			
Checking account	$ 500		
Savings	5,500	Liabilities	
Stock at current		Personal loan	$ 2,000
market value	8,000	Owner's equity	12,000
Total assets	$14,000	Total equities	$14,000

AFTER PURCHASE

Assets		Equities	
Cash		Liabilities	
Checking account	$ 500	Personal loan	$ 2,000
Stock	3,500	Mortgage loan	30,000
House	40,000	Owner's equity	12,000
Total assets	$44,000	Total equities	$44,000

Consider an additional point. We have said that two groups can have claims on assets—creditors and owners. Creditors are legally entitled to the first claim, and the balance that remains is the owner's equity. Thus, neither the creditors, nor the owners, nor the two groups together can have total claims on the assets that are in excess of the *total* assets. We come, therefore, to the observation that *assets must always equal equities,* or (since equities may take the form of liabilities and also owner's equity) *assets must also always equal liabilities plus owner's equity.*

This equation is often referred to as the basic accounting equation, and is sometimes called the "dual aspect principle." All business transactions are recorded in terms of their dual effect on assets and equities.

Our illustration involved a single business transaction—the purchase of a home. The two aspects of this transaction were:

1. To show an increase in our assets in the amount of $30,000, with an equal increase in equities (creditor's equities) in the same amount. (All accounting systems based on the dual aspect principle are of necessity described as "double-entry bookkeeping systems.")

2. To point out in general terms three basic concepts: assets as things of measurable monetary value; liabilities as creditor's claims against assets; and owner's equities as the claims of owners on assets.

Let's take these same concepts and, using exactly the same approach, see how they apply in a highly simplified business situation involving Gerry M.'s Furniture Mart.

Gerry has decided to open his own furniture store. To do this, he plans to use his personal cash savings in the amount of $15,000. If Gerry goes into business on July 27, 1974, his accountant will describe the balance of Gerry's assets and equities as follows:

GERRY M.'S FURNITURE MART
Balance of Assets and Equities
July 27, 1974

Assets		Equities	
Cash	$15,000	Owner's equity	$15,000

If, on July 30, Gerry purchases a delivery truck, the accountant will show this revised situation as follows:

GERRY M.'S FURNITURE MART
Balance of Assets and Equities
July 30, 1974

Assets		Equities	
Cash	$10,000	Owner's equity	$15,000
Delivery truck	5,000		
Total assets	$15,000		

By applying the same concepts we used in our home-purchase illustration, Gerry's accountant has prepared a financial evaluation of Gerry's new business on July 27 and July 30 showing the balance of the assets and equities of the business as it stood on these dates.

In accounting, such a statement is called a "balance sheet." It is one of two basic accounting documents used to report on the financial condition of a company. (The other is the income statement—about which, more later on.) Its name is well chosen, since it (1) always shows a balance of assets and equities, and (2) must always balance assets and equities, as we've already seen from the dual aspect concept.

Under normal business circumstances, the balance of assets and equities being reported in a balance sheet is constantly changing. Thus a balance sheet can reflect the status of assets and equities only at a given moment. For this reason, the balance sheet is always dated, and that date is critical to a clear understanding of the financial information being presented.

Most companies usually prepare a formal balance sheet at least once a year, usually as of the end of the year. Clearly, the elementary nature of Gerry's financial affairs simplifies the preparation of a balance sheet in his business; however, the same basic concepts are used whatever the size or complexity of the business.

THE ACCRUAL CONCEPT

A second basic accounting concept—the accrual principle—is related to another basic accounting document, the income statement.

The accrual concept is a rather nettlesome notion, since most of us tend to conduct our personal financial affairs on a cash rather than an accrual basis. We tend to view our personal financial situation in light of how much cash or how many other liquid assets we have on hand. Similarly, we think of our annual net income on a gross basis, or at best after taxes; we never, however, deduct the real depreciation on our automobile or the wear and tear associated with the use of household and personal effects. Depreciation will be discussed later on; for now, let's return to Gerry M. and continue to record the development of his new furniture mart. The initial three transactions (of which you have already seen two) result in simplified balance sheets as shown below.

Event: July 27. Gerry M. decides to enter the furniture business and invests $15,000 of his personal savings.

GERRY M.'S FURNITURE MART
Balance Sheet
July 27, 1974

Assets		Equities	
Cash	$15,000	Owner's equity	$15,000

Event: July 30. Gerry M. purchases a new delivery truck for his business.

GERRY M.'S FURNITURE MART
Balance Sheet
July 30, 1974

Assets		Equities	
Cash	$10,000	Owner's equity	$15,000
Delivery truck	5,000		
Total assets	$15,000		

Event: August 6. Gerry M. obtains a $5,000 bank loan for his new business.

GERRY M.'S FURNITURE MART
Balance Sheet
August 6, 1974

Assets		Equities	
		Liabilities	
Cash	$15,000	Bank loan	$ 5,000
Delivery truck	5,000	Owner's equity	15,000
Total assets	$20,000	Total equities	$20,000

Let's continue this process with comments on the transactions that follow.

Event: September 6. Gerry M. purchases, with cash, $6,000 worth of merchandise to be resold. (Merchandise purchased or manufactured by a business and held for eventual sale is called "inventory.")

GERRY M.'S FURNITURE MART
Balance Sheet
September 6, 1974

Assets		Equities	
Cash	$ 9,000	Liabilities	
Merchandise inventory	6,000	Bank loan	$ 5,000
Delivery truck	5,000	Owner's equity	15,000
Total assets	$20,000	Total equities	$20,000

Event: September 8. Gerry M. sells for $600 (cash) merchandise that cost $500.

Since this particular transaction presents a slightly new wrinkle involving Gerry's first sale (the exchange of goods for a price), let's follow its effect on the balance sheet step by step.

The effect on assets is relatively clear-cut. The cash asset increases from $9,000 to $9,600 as a result of cash received from the sale. On the other hand, inventory decreases by the amount of $500 (the cost of the merchandise sold). The other asset, the truck, remains unchanged at $5,000. So, in total, Gerry M.'s assets now amount to $20,100:

Assets

Cash	$ 9,600
Inventory	5,500
Truck	5,000
Total assets	$20,100

On the equity side of the balance sheet, the liability of a $5,000 loan, payable to the bank, remains unchanged. At first glance, owner's equity of $15,000 would also appear to remain the same. If so, however, the total equities of $20,000 would be less than the assets of $20,100. For the basic accounting equation to match, total equities must also equal $20,100. We can see why they should. The bank's claim of $5,000 on the assets has not changed. There are $15,100 of assets to be claimed, and these can now be claimed only by the owner. Gerry's equity—his owner's equity—has increased by $100. The reason, of course, is that the $500 asset of merchandise was exchanged for another asset, cash of $600. All these changes result in a September 8 balance sheet that looks like this:

GERRY M.'S FURNITURE MART
Balance Sheet
September 8, 1974

Assets		Equities	
Cash	$ 9,600	Liabilities	
Merchandise inventory	5,500	Bank loan	$ 5,000
Delivery truck	5,000	Owner's equity	15,100
Total assets	$20,100	Total equities	$20,100

13

Event: September 10. Gerry M. purchases $2,000 of merchandise and agrees to pay for it within sixty days.

In this transaction, Gerry charges his purchase as we might charge a personal purchase at a department store. It represents a liability since we do not own the merchandise. This particular type of liability is called an "account payable" and appears on this balance sheet:

GERRY M.'S FURNITURE MART
Balance Sheet
September 10, 1974

Assets		Equities	
		Liabilities	
Cash	$ 9,600	Accounts payable	$ 2,000
Merchandise inventory	7,500	Bank loan	5,000
Delivery truck	5,000	Owner's equity	15,100
Total assets	$22,100	Total equities	$22,100

Event: September 12. Gerry M. sells for $800 merchandise that cost $600. The customer agrees to pay the total amount in thirty days.

The reader will recognize that the effect of this transaction is the same as that which took place on September 8. The only difference is that instead of receiving cash outright, the furniture mart has received the promise of payment within thirty days. Although not cash, this promise represents an asset which is called an "account receivable." It appears in this Balance Sheet:

GERRY M.'S FURNITURE MART
Balance Sheet
September 12, 1974

Assets		Equities	
Cash	$ 9,600	Liabilities	
Accounts receivable	800	Accounts payable	$ 2,000
Merchandise inventory	6,900	Bank loan	5,000
Delivery truck	5,000	Owner's equity	15,300
Total assets	$22,300	Total equities	$22,300

Event: September 15. Gerry M. sells $1,000 of merchandise that cost $700. The customer pays cash.

Here again, this transaction affects owner's equity in the same manner as the sales on September 8 and 12.

Let's stop now to look at the following comparison of the original versus the last balance sheet for the furniture mart.

GERRY M.'S FURNITURE MART
Comparative Balance Sheet

Assets	July 27	Sept. 15	Equities	July 27	Sept. 15
Cash	$15,000	$10,600	Liabilities		
Accounts receivable		800	Accounts payable		$ 2,000
Inventory		6,200	Loan payable		5,000
Delivery truck		5,000	Subtotal		$ 7,000
Total assets	$15,000	$22,600	Owner's equity	$15,000	15,600
			Total equities	$15,000	$22,600

The furniture mart has increased its assets and equities by $7,600. Second, and more important, owner's equity has increased by $600. This occurred because the assets of merchandise were exchanged for another asset—cash—at a higher value. In accounting terms, such an increase in owner's equity is called "income" or "profit." When an accountant refers to income, he is concerned exclusively with increases in owner's equity.

Actually, only three transactions of the furniture mart had an effect on owner's equity. These were the sales of merchandise on September 8, 12, and 15. On the 8th and 15th, owner's equity increased at the same time cash increased because the customer paid money for his merchandise. On September 12, however, equity increased while cash remained unchanged because the customer bought the merchandise on credit. We can see that increases in owner's equity do not depend on increases or decreases in cash.

These sales increased the owner's equity. In accounting, an increase in owner's equity is called "revenue." The process of turning the goods over to the customer, however, brought about a decrease in the owner's equity in the amount that was paid for the goods sold. This decrease in owner's equity is called an "expense." The difference between the revenue (an increase in owner's equity) and the expense (the decrease in owner's equity) is "net income."

The distinctive aspect of the three business transactions that affected owner's equity was not whether cash increased or decreased, but whether revenues were greater than expenses. The concept that net income is measured by increases or decreases in owner's equity rather than by increases or decreases in cash is called the "accrual concept."

The dual aspect concept has particular relevance to the first fundamental accounting document—the balance sheet. The accrual concept is basic to the second fundamental accounting document—the income statement.

We can summarize our comments on the conceptual basis for an income statement as follows:

- In accounting, increases in owner's equity that arise from the sale and exchange of a good or service are called net income.
- When a business provides a good or service, the monies it receives increase owner's equity and are called revenues.
- The costs that business incurs to provide the good or service decrease the owner's equity and are called expenses.
- Under the accrual concept, net income is measured by the difference between revenues and expenses, *not* by increases or decreases in cash.

An income statement summarizes the revenues and expenses of a business over a given period of time and reflects the difference between the two as net income if revenues are greater than expenses. If expenses are greater than revenues, there has not been a net income to the owners, and the result is shown as a net loss.

A term that is often used interchangeably with "net income" is "profit." Thus an income statement is also referred to as a "statement of profit and/or loss" (often abbreviated P/L Statement). The choice is only one of terminology, since the purpose and concept of the statement are the same under either label.

An income statement for Gerry M.'s Furniture Mart for the period between July 27 and September 15 would appear as follows:

GERRY M.'S FURNITURE MART
Income Statement
Period Ending September 15, 1974

Revenues	$2,400
Less cost of goods sold	1,800
Net income	$ 600

The source of these figures is as follows:

Revenues (increases in owner's equity through sales of merchandise)		Expenses (decreases in owner's equity for the costs associated with providing the goods)	
September 8	$ 600	September 8	$ 500
September 12	800	September 12	600
September 15	1,000	September 15	700
Total revenues as per income statement	$2,400	Total expenses as per income statement	$1,800

Revenues minus expenses equal net income, or $600. Our income statement shows the same net increase to owner's equity as the comparison of the balance sheets of the furniture mart for July 27 and September 15 (page 15). This is as expected, since net income represents the increase in owner's equity that takes place through the conduct of a company's business.

In theory, the total net income of a business over its entire life is simply the amount the owners get out of it versus what they originally put in. It is possible to measure the net income of business this way. The owner's equity could be calculated after ten years of business activity and compared with the owner's original equity. If there has been an increase, as there should have been, this would be the net income of the business for the total 10-year period. Although an accountant could measure the net income of a business this way, it is impractical for two reasons:

1. Neither management nor the owners of a business can wait until the 10-year period is over to see how the business has fared.

2. Management and owners want to know more specifically *when* the increase in owner's equity occurred. For example, has it occurred evenly over the life of the business, in the beginning, or at the end?

For these reasons, determinations of net income—in the form of income statements—are made at frequent intervals over the life of the business. In most countries it is customary (and, in some, mandatory) for businesses to prepare an income statement at least once a year. Almost all publicly held corporations in the United States prepare income statements for each calendar quarter and issue them to the public and to their shareholders. For its own internal use, management may have income statements prepared on a monthly basis.

Our accounting efforts on behalf of Gerry M. obviously remain simple; and although we have touched on only the fundamentals of an income statement, we have a foundation on which to build later in the series. First, however, a few more basics.

OTHER BASIC CONCEPTS

Five significant but less important principles also explain the work of the accountant:

• The Money Measurement Principle. This principle says that accounting measures business transactions *only* in terms of money. This idea has several advantages. First, it provides a simple measuring device that allows a variety of different facts to be expressed in a common denominator. For example, a large steel plant can be compared with a research laboratory when both are expressed in monetary terms. Second, things that are expressed in monetary terms can be dealt with mathematically to express various aspects of the business.

But although the money measurement principle brings obvious and necessary advantages to the accounting process, it simultaneously imposes severe limitations, since the most valuable assets of a business are often intangible. Perhaps the best example of this fact is the great but intangible value of the skills of employees and management. No one has yet devised a way to quantify these skills in terms of money. Other important assets unaccountable for in monetary terms include technological know-how, reputation, brand awareness, and so on.

A recognition that accounting reports may ignore some of the most important facets of a business is the beginning of the wise and intelligent use of accounting information.

• The Business Entity Principle. The business entity principle is another rather simple notion. It means that accounting keeps records for business entities rather than for individuals.

If, for example, Gerry M. withdraws $150 from his furniture mart's checking account, he is $150 richer, the business has $150 less, and there has been no overall change in Gerry's total cash position. However, the accountant would record only the effect of this transaction (−$150) on the business and ignore the effect of this transaction on Gerry. Transactions, therefore, can affect the owner of a business in one way and the business itself in another way.

• The Going Concern Principle. Most businesses begin with the basic idea that they will be operated in a logical, rational manner that will lead to success over an extended period of time. The same basic assumption is made by the accountant and is called the "going concern principle." It facilitates the accountant's difficult job of assessing values. To see why this is so, we must discuss the cost concept.

• The Cost Concept. Cost, as we all know, doesn't necessarily equal value. A dramatic illustration of this occurred in the bull market of December 1970, when various investors were willing to pay $320 for a share of equity in IBM Corporation even though the value of its assets was only $52 per share. The cost concept has its problems and limitations, but no one in the accounting profession has yet been able to come up with an acceptable alternative that provides the same practicality and objectivity.

Earlier, we saw that a basic function of an accountant is to list assets in preparing a balance sheet. But how is the value of these assets established? The answer is not as clear-cut as it might appear.

To illustrate, let's again use an example of home ownership. Suppose one morning a prospective buyer looks at your home and asks you what you consider to be its value. Later on in the day, a tax assessor comes to look at your home and asks the same question. Most of us would give one answer to the prospective buyer and another to the tax assessor, whether or not we are honest enough to admit it. The point is that the assessment of value can be a highly subjective process to which an accountant must bring objectivity. There are several possible ways to value business assets:

1. Value them at their market value. Simple enough—just state the worth of the property today. But this isn't always as easy as it sounds. The value of something can be highly dependent upon the prospective purchaser's particular needs. For this reason, it's possible to get three, four, or five differing evaluations of the worth of any particular property. The economists call this the theory of "utility." However, if the accountant were to use this concept, he would again run directly into the problem of subjectivity.

2. Value the assets on the basis of the amount of money required to replace them. This replacement value does away with a value range that depends on the prospective buyer's needs. However, the cost of replacing something often depends on *how* it is replaced. For

GERRY M.'s FURNITURE MART
Application of the Realization Principle

Date	Transaction	Amount	Effect on Cash	Effect on Revenue
December 31	Cash sale and delivery same day	$200	$200	$200
December 31	Credit sale and delivery same day	300	0	300
December 31	Payment received in advance for delivery next year	400	400	0
	Totals	$900	$600	$500

example, the costs of replacing a structure can vary depending on who does the work, what material they use, how efficiently they go about the construction, and other factors. The use of a replacement approach will almost surely provide a range rather than a single common value to place on the asset.

3. Determine the value of any particular asset on the basis of its original cost. This is certainly one cost that you and others could agree on. You need only produce the original invoice. This doesn't mean, however, that everyone would agree you had made a good buy. The primary appeal of this "cost concept" is its expediency and objectivity. But, in line with the going concern principle, it is assumed that the assets will be used in the normal conduct of the business rather than sold or disposed of. So the question of the value of assets is not as critical as it might otherwise be.

● The Realization Principle. According to this principle, revenue from a sale is not realized when a sales contract is made, or when the order is placed, or when the merchandise is manufactured, or when it is paid for; it is realized *only when it is delivered to and accepted by the customer.*

The realization principle, like the cost principle, is an effort to make accounting more objective. The accountant says, in effect, "It is not until a deal is wrapped up and sealed, and the merchandise or services delivered, that I will consider a company to have obtained revenue."

There is a similarity between the realization principle and the accrual principle. The application of the accrual principle showed that, in accounting, increases or decreases in cash do not necessarily determine the net income of a business. Let's apply the realization principle to Gerry M.'s Furniture Mart.

The simple table on the opposite page summarizes three transactions made on December 31.

Obviously, application of the realization principle may result in situations where the net income of the business can be affected without a corresponding effect on cash.

Clearly, too, accounting principles are by no means scientifically derived. They are man-made agreements that serve as practical aids to solving accounting problems. But although the use of these principles provides a common, accepted approach to the measurement of financial results of a business, there are still an incredible number of ways in which financial results can be presented. ■

Related Reading: AMACOM Books

BASIC FINANCIAL MANAGEMENT by Curtis W. Symonds (1969). Deals with such fundamental questions as What is the nature of invested capital? How is capital paid for? How does capital affect profit?

THE MEANINGFUL INTERPRETATION OF FINANCIAL STATEMENTS (revised edition) by Donald E. Miller (1972). Explains how 15 key financial relationships can give you a sharp picture of any company's financial standing.

A GUIDE TO CAPITAL EXPENDITURE ANALYSIS by Moustafa H. Abdelsamad (1973). Describes the most popular techniques for deciding which opportunities should receive the scarce resources of money, executive time, personnel, and space.

A DESIGN FOR BUSINESS INTELLIGENCE by Curtis W. Symonds (1971). Explores the differing needs for management information within an organization, and explains why the manager should not let computer experts decide what kind of information he should get.

Part 2: A closer look at balance sheets and income statements

There is an old story about a successful applicant for the job of chief accountant. After many others had been turned away, he was hired because he answered the president's question, "How much is two and two?" by replying, "How much do you want it to be, Sir?"

Businesses do account for their results in a variety of ways. For example, almost all companies can obtain discounts for prompt payment. One firm may take these discounts and reduce the cost of merchandise; another may take discounts and record them as income realized on prompt payments.

ACCOUNTING PRINCIPLES

These are but two of many ways in which accounting information can be recorded—all of them in accordance with the principles we have been discussing. Accounting makes an effort to overcome this deficiency through the use of three so-called accepted, basic accounting conventions: consistency, conservatism, and materiality.

• The Convention of Consistency. This convention states that once a business transaction is accounted for in one particular manner, it must be accounted for in this same way consistently thereafter. If, for example, a company accounts for cash discounts as income derived from prompt payment, it must continue to do so in all succeeding statements of income. This doctrine makes it very difficult for a business to manipulate its figures by showing them in a favorable light on one occasion and then, when it is convenient, changing to another approach. The convention of consistency is the basis, in annual audit reports, of the statement that reads to the effect, "This statement has been prepared in accordance with generally accepted accounting principles, on a basis *consistent* with the preceding year."

• The Convention of Conservatism. In Part 1, we discussed the inherently objective and conservative nature of the cost and realization concepts. The convention of conservatism is merely an amplification of this approach. That is, whenever the accountant is given the option to do so, he will always choose to reflect financial data in terms of the lower of two possible values.

Perhaps the best example of this occurs in the evaluation of inventories (merchandise held by the company for sale). At the close of the accounting period, the accountant, as we know from the cost concept, would value this inventory on the basis of its cost to the business. But if its market value at this point were now lower than its original cost, the accountant would, in accordance with the convention of conservatism, reflect the lower value. Without exception, accounting statements employ this approach in the evaluation of inventories, and it is sometimes called "the cost or market value, whichever is lower." We can see that it grows naturally out of the convention of conservatism.

In accounting for gains and losses from the sale of property, "sound" accounting will invariably recognize any loss that has occurred or could possibly occur, but never any profit on the sale of assets until the sale actually takes place. The major objective of the convention of conservatism, like that of consistency, is to protect the shareholders or owners of a business from a fraudulent or misleading representation of the worth of the business.

• The Convention of Materiality. When a particular transaction is not material to the financial results of the business, the accountant can use his own discretion as to when and perhaps how to record that event. Theoretically, each time a piece of paper, a typewriter ribbon, or a pencil is used, it becomes an expense. As a practical matter, nothing could be more ridiculous (or costly, for that matter) than to account for expenses so precisely. Common sense, as well as the convention of materiality, allows the accountant to take only the total costs for the month or even an average of several months' costs of supplies as the expense.

Although this convention is useful in simplifying the accountant's work, the nonfinancial manager should make sure that what is material or immaterial to the accountant is also material or immaterial to management (and shareholders).

Now that we have covered the fundamental principles and conventions of accounting, let us look in greater depth and detail at the two basic accounting statements, the balance sheet and the income statement.

In the view of a business as a continuum of events over a period of time, there are two kinds of events: First, there are those that change only the status and balance of assets or liabilities. These involve the exchange of one asset for another or an increase in liabilities in exchange for assets. They affect only accounts on a balance sheet and are balance-sheet transactions. Second, there are transactions that affect not only the status of assets and liabilities, but also the status of revenue and expense accounts. They are income statement transactions.

The work of the accountant may be compared with that of the photographer. Both record events, the photographer with his camera and the accountant with his ledger.

The similarity between a balance sheet and a photographic snapshot is clear. A snapshot captures a situation only at the moment in time when the picture is taken. So, too, many business actions take place before and after the balance sheet is drawn up. The balance sheet, too, is a still life—a static report on the business at a particular moment.

The income statement is similar to another type of photography. The income statement is a mechanism that accumulates the effect of each day's transactions. In the case of Gerry M.'s business, the income statement accumulated the sales for one day, then another, and so on, so that the total sales transacted up to the date the income statement was prepared were reflected in that statement. Thus an income statement captures and amasses in one record everything that goes on in a business *over a period of time*. In this way, it is like the motion picture.

Although our analogy to photography demonstrates some of the basic differences between the income statement and the balance sheet, it is important to clearly understand the close relationship between them. Let's look again at the balance sheets and income statements we prepared for Gerry M. These are given in Exhibit 1 on page 27, which shows that the increase in owner's equity between July 27 and September 15 is exactly the same amount shown as the net income on the income statement for the same period.

If Gerry had taken $200 of the net income of the business before preparing the balance sheet on September 15, 1974, this amount would have had to be reflected in the balance sheet and would have modified the owner's equity section of the balance sheet in this way:

Owner's equity	$600
Less drawings	200
Net owner's equity	$400

Under these circumstances, the increase in owner's equity from one balance sheet to another would be equal to the net income for the period less any net income drawn by Gerry M.

THE BALANCE SHEET

With some of these general ideas in mind, let's turn to a more detailed examination of the basic structure and terminology of the balance sheet and income statement. The balance sheets prepared for Gerry M. have been purposely brief and simple. For a larger, more complex business, they would of course need to be expanded. Also, the shareholders and managers of a business are often interested in a greater amount of detail. In a standard balance sheet format for the presentation of a business's basic financial data, assets are subdivided into three major categories: current assets, fixed assets, and other assets.

Exhibit 1.

Relationship between balance sheets and income statement for Gerry M.'s Furniture Mart.

BALANCE SHEET July 27, 1974				BALANCE SHEET September 15, 1974	
Cash	*Owner's Equity*	*Assets*		*Liabilities and Owner's Equity*	
$15,000	$15,000	Cash	$10,600	Accounts payable	$ 2,000
		Accounts receivable	800	Loans payable	5,000
		Inventory	6,200	Total liabilities	$ 7,000
		Delivery truck	5,000	Owner's equity	15,600
		Total	$22,600	Total	$22,600

OWNER'S EQUITY

July 27	*September 15*	*Increase*
$15,000	$15,600	$600

INCOME STATEMENT
September 15, 1974

Revenues	$2,400
Less cost of goods sold	1,800
Net increase	$ 600

• **Current Assets.** The four items described below are the most common forms of current assets, although there could be others. (Assets are classified as current as long as they are cash, or can be converted into cash, within the customary operating period of the business—usually one year.)

Cash. This usually represents the funds on hand or readily available in checking accounts. Not included: cash funds legally tied up, such as funds held in special deposits or in escrow.

Marketable securities. These represent temporary investments in the stocks or bonds in other businesses or enterprises, and possibly governmental bonds. Next to cash, they are usually the most liquid assets, and can be turned into cash on short notice.

Accounts receivable. These represent monies owed to the firm by customers for the purchase of merchandise bought on credit. Accounts receivable are often shown as a gross amount of accounts receivable, and then a "reserve for doubtful accounts" is shown as a deduction. This reserve represents an estimate of accounts receivable on which the business does not expect to be able to collect.

(We will discuss the accounting of doubtful accounts receivable in more detail later on.)

Inventories. Inventories represent purchased merchandise being held in stock until it is resold. When a business manufactures its own product for sale, inventories include the value of the merchandise or product manufactured and being held for sale. Inventories also include the raw materials that go into the product and products in the process of being manufactured. Inventories are often shown in this order: raw-material inventories, goods-in-process inventories, and finished-goods inventories.

Prepaid expenses. These expenses, paid in advance by the business, constitute a right to a future service not yet used by the business. A common example: the insurance coverage a business pays for in advance of receiving services.

• Fixed Assets. These are tangible, permanent investments in so-called capital facilities (usually brick and mortar) or equipment. Many balance sheets much more descriptively and accurately label them "property," "plant," and "equipment." Almost all these fixed assets are shown in the following order in the balance sheet: gross fixed assets, reserve for accumulated depreciation, and net fixed assets.

The term "gross fixed assets" refers to the original value; that is, the cost incurred to purchase or construct the physical facility (note the application of the cost concept). Gross fixed assets are reduced by an item called reserve for accumulated depreciation. Depreciation is a major accounting concept in itself, to be discussed in detail later on. For now, let's define depreciation as an estimate of how much the original value of all company assets has decreased because of usage, passage of time, obsolescence, or a combination of these. This amount is deducted from the gross fixed assets to arrive at the figure for net fixed assets, which is the value (that is, the cost) of the fixed assets diminished by the depreciation accumulated to the date of the financial statement.

• Other Assets. These include various assets not readily classifiable as either current or fixed. Other assets, like fixed assets, tend to be long-term ones. The most common of these is investments. A company can have marketable securities that are also investments. But investments shown under *other assets* usually differ in several respects from marketable securities. First, they are intended to be held for an extended period of time—at least one year or longer. Second, they are being held to control the company owned or to earn a significant return on the holding, or both.

28

Intangible assets. These are a common form of other assets. They include patents, copyrights, franchises, and similar matters. They can have a significant value in generating income, but are distinct from the tangibility of, say, a plant.

Liabilities and shareholders' equities. The right-hand side of the balance sheet consists of the claims on the assets of a corporation: (1) liabilities through the claims of the creditors, and (2) claims of the owners, or owner's equities. The liabilities and owner's equities sections of a balance sheet are also broken down into standard sub-classficiations: current liabilities, long-term liabilities, and shareholders' equity.

• Current Liabilities. These include obligations expected to fall due within the next accounting period (usually the next year). This particular definition is similar to the definition of current assets. The most common types of current liabilities are described below.

Accounts payable. Accounts payable represent the counterpart of accounts receivable. With an account payable, the business is a debtor rather than a creditor—with a legal obligation to make a payment.

Notes payable. Notes payable are similar to accounts payable. Usually, the legal instrument associated with this obligation is much more formal and will involve a longer period of time for payment. A note payable has its converse in the note receivable, shown on the left-hand side of the balance sheet as an asset.

Accrued liabilities. Under law, the term "accrue" means to become a present right or enforceable demand. In accounting, the term is used similarly, and accrued liabilities represent business obligations not yet paid for. Such obligations can take several forms and may or may not be indicated separately on the balance sheet. One of the most common to be shown separately is accrued taxes, which could include federal, state, or local income taxes as well as real estate taxes.

• Long-Term Liabilities. Long-term liabilities include debts (or claims on assets) that fall due a year or longer in the future. They are usually incurred to obtain more permanent funds for the business and are often shown according to the source of funds, as described below.

Bank loans. Funds obtained from bank loans can be either a short- or a long-term liability. If they are due and payable within one year from the date of the balance sheet, they are classified as a short-term liability. Those payable in more than a year are classified as a long-term liability.

Bonds. These are another form of long-term capital. Bonds are often obtained from many people who are given certificates, called "bonds," as evidence of a loan. Bonds usually have extended 15- to 20-year repayment periods.

- <u>Shareholders' Equity</u>. The lower left-hand section of the balance sheet contains the shareholders' (or owner's) equity section. Shareholders' equities represent the claim of owners on assets after the obligations to all other creditors have been fulfilled. There are usually two basic forms of shareholders' equity, as described below.

Common stock. Common stock (or capital stock) represents the original contribution to the business made by the owners in order to purchase assets and conduct business affairs. In the case of an individual proprietorship, such as that of Gerry M., this contribution represents the original amount of funds he put into the business. In the case of a corporation, the contribution may be a large number of shares sold to thousands of individual investors through an established public stock exchange.

Retained earnings. The retained earnings of the business represent the total cumulative net income that a business earns over its life, less any funds that have been returned to the owners in the form of dividends. We showed the buildup of retained earnings for a period of one year for Gerry M. in Exhibit 1. In the past, the term "earned surplus" was frequently used to describe the retained earnings of a business. It is appropriately falling into disuse, since "surplus" is misleading. The funds are not surplus—because they have been ploughed back into the business to provide monies for expansion and growth.

THE INCOME STATEMENT

Assets used to be the determining factor in the worth of a business—so investors' and shareholders' attention focused primarily on a company's balance sheet. Times have changed, however, and the American investor now emphasizes the so-called growth potential of the corporation. Generally, this is the ability of a corporation to sustain a constantly increasing rate of growth in net income year after year. This change has switched attention from the balance sheet to the income statement. Let's look at a typical income statement, as shown in Exhibit 2.

- <u>Sales</u>. The first item on this income statement is "sales." Sometimes this item is called "sales revenue" or just "revenue"—but, whatever its title, it refers to the amounts received (or to be received

—accounts receivable) for goods or services provided (or, under the realization principle, delivered) to other organizations in the conduct of its business for the period shown.

Exhibit 2. A typical income statement for the year ended 1973.

Sales	$3,100,000
Less cost of goods sold	2,350,000
Gross profit	$ 750,000
Less operating expenses	
Selling expenses	250,000
Administrative expenses	200,000
Operating profit	$300,000
Provision for income taxes	$144,000
Net income	$156,000

• Cost of Goods Sold. As in our illustration, it is usually shown as "less cost of goods sold" since it is deducted from "sales." The term had the same meaning when we used it to prepare Gerry M.'s income statement. It represents what it cost the business to either purchase or manufacture the goods sold in order to generate the revenues in the first line, "sales." In most businesses, cost of goods sold represents the most significant item of expense for the business. For this reason, it is almost always shown as a separate item.

• Gross Profit. The subtraction of "cost of goods sold" from "sales" leaves a remainder called "gross profit." Gross profit is almost invariably shown as a separate item on an income statement. It indicates the income that remains to cover the expenses of selling the product and administering the business. These two expenses are shown next as "operating expenses"—the expenses incurred to operate the business for the period of the income statement. Sometimes they are shown as a single item or subdivided, as in our illustration, into the two major components, "selling expenses" and "administrative expenses." Selling expenses include the costs of sales organization, sales promotions, and similar factors. Administrative expenses cover the cost of managing the organization and typically include insurance costs, rent, heat, light, accounting, legal costs, and so on.

• Operating Profit. Operating expenses reduce the amount of the company's gross profit and must be covered before net income can be generated. The deduction of operating expenses from gross profit leaves the business's "operating profit," which is shown as another separate subtotal and represents profit that has been provided from the normal operations of the business. Many income statements make a distinction between operating and nonoperating profits in order to differentiate the net income generated as a result of the normal, routine conduct of the business from the net income generated by sale of equipment or property or some other similar transaction not normally considered the basic function of the business. Sometimes operating profit is described as "net income before taxes."

• Income Taxes. The "provision for income taxes," a significant item for reducing business income, is almost always shown separately.

• Net Income. This, the final line on the income statement, is, of course, the most critical piece of information—the final net result of operating the business for the period covered. Net income, as we have stressed before, represents the increment (or if there is a net loss, the decrement) that has resulted from successful operation of the business for the period of time covered.

Balance sheets and income statements are the output of accounting systems. We turn next to a more detailed discussion of special accounting problems and concepts involved in obtaining this output.

SPECIAL ACCOUNTING PROBLEMS

Let's look at three special accounting problems: (1) fixed assets accounting, which includes depreciation costs; (2) inventory accounting, which is the cost-of-goods-sold determination; and (3) accounts receivable, which is accounting for bad debts. These three areas are given special attention for two reasons. First, they involve some concepts, procedures, and terminology critical to the proper understanding and utilization of financial data. Second, they include areas that the nonfinancial manager finds difficult to understand.

1. Fixed Assets. Earlier, we defined fixed assets as permanent investments of a long-term nature in so-called capital facilities. These include property, plant, and equipment that will be used by the business to provide goods or services.

• Recording Original Value. The first logical question concerning fixed asset accounting is: On what basis should their value be recorded? The application of the cost principle gives the answer to this question—which is cost. The next question then becomes: Exactly· what makes up the cost? The answer has become well defined in accounting practice and can be summarized as follows:

a. The cost of fixed assets includes all costs of obtaining and installing the fixed assets. In the purchase of a piece of machinery, for instance, costs of transportation and installation are included in the fixed cost. Thus the basic cost of the machinery might be $1,000, but there is an additional $200 installation cost and a $100 freight charge. The total cost of the fixed asset is recorded on the books as $1,300.

b. A business may construct a machine or a building, using its own labor for the partial construction or installation. The costs to the company for this labor are included as part of the asset.

c. A business may pay for a new asset, partly in cash and partly in the value of the old assets traded in. For example, if a business pays $500 cash for a calculating machine that has a trade-in value of $300, the total real cost of the new calculating machine is $800, not $500, and $800 is the figure used to record the total cost of the asset.

• <u>Depreciation</u>. We have said that fixed assets include property, plant, and equipment that will be used by the business to provide goods or services. The buildings, equipment, and machinery used for this purpose day after day will obviously wear out and ultimately become useless. As this process takes place, the original value of the asset decreases, with a corresponding reduction in the owner's equity. To understand this process, consider the following example:

<u>Event</u>. A delivery service is started with the $5,000 purchase of a delivery truck by the owner.

Balance Sheet
Delivery Service
Beginning of Year

Assets		*Equities*	
Fixed assets	$5,000	Owner's equity	$5,000

<u>Event</u>. Delivery service is operated for a year, but the truck now has less value, since it is older and has been used. The truck now has a value of only $3,500.

Balance Sheet
Delivery Service
End of Year

Assets		Equities	
Fixed assets	$3,500	Owner's equity	$3,500

In this example, reduction in the asset value has been taken as a direct deduction to owner's equity. We know, however, that under regular procedures this would be done by reflecting the amount as an expense (which is also a reduction of owner's equity) in an income statement. The process of taking the estimated usage of an asset each year and charging it as an expense against the business is called "depreciation." However, not all fixed assets are depreciated. Fixed assets include land as well as plant and equipment. The value of land tends to be permanent. When it is used as a building site (rather than being mined or farmed), it does not wear out. In fact, it tends to appreciate in value. So the accountant does not depreciate land.

Other types of fixed assets do wear out, and to calculate the expense associated with this depreciation, the accountant has to determine three facts:

1. The original cost of the asset—usually determined in accordance with the principles set forth earlier.
2. The estimated life of the asset.
3. The estimated residual or scrap value, if any, of the asset at the end of its life.

Let's apply these three factors to determine the depreciation of a fixed asset—remembering that our objective is to determine the *estimated usage* of the asset and to record it as an expense during the period of its use.

Assume that a business purchases a machine with a basic factory cost of $1,000—with an additional $100 of costs to deliver it and another $100 to install it on the premises. Applying the guidelines we have just discussed, we can readily determine that the total original cost of the fixed asset would be $1,200.

The next step is to determine the estimated salvage value. The word "estimated" here is critical because, of course, this can be nothing more than an educated guess on what the machine will be worth at the time of disposal. Let's assume that on the basis of past experience and/or consultation with used-machinery dealers, the accountant tags the final estimated salvage value at $200. Now that we have the original cost of the fixed asset as well as the estimated salvage value, we can determine the estimated net cost of the asset, which is simply the difference between these two—or $1,000.

The next step is to determine the estimated useful life. There are a variety of sources from which to obtain this. One of the most common is the guidelines issued by the Internal Revenue Service. Others are engineering, equipment, manpower, and other associations. Assume that we arrive at an estimate of four years. We now have all three elements we need to arrive at our estimated annual depreciation expense, which we can calculate to be $250 per year. This is obtained by dividing the estimated net cost of the fixed asset, that is, the original $1,200 of cost less the estimated salvage value of $200, by the useful life period of four years, as shown below:

Purchase price of asset	$1,000
Delivery cost	100
Installation cost	100
Total cost of asset	$1,200
Less estimated salvage value	200
Asset cost to be depreciated	$1,000

$$\frac{\$1,000 \text{ (asset cost to be depreciated)}}{4 \text{ years}} = \$250 \text{ per year}$$

If we were to plot this process graphically, it would appear as shown in Exhibit 3.

Because this process (depreciating the estimated net cost of the fixed asset in equal annual amounts of depreciation expense) results in a straight line, it is called "the straight-line method of depreciation." Simple in conception and application, it is the most commonly used approach in American business.

But because assets do not always necessarily wear out or obsolesce at the same rate each year, two different so-called accelerated methods of depreciation have been developed during the last fifteen years and have become accepted accounting practice. They are described below.

Sum-of-the-Years Digits. The formula for calculating sum-of-the-years-digits depreciation is a fraction, with the numerator representing the years of remaining useful life of the asset and the denominator indicating the sum of the digits of the years of estimated useful life. Using this approach, we would depreciate the machine with a net asset value of $1,000 in the following way:

35

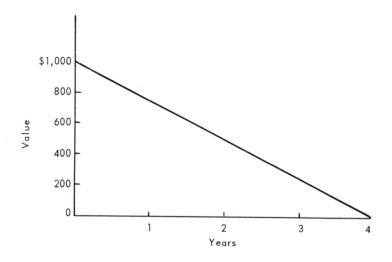

Exhibit 3. Straight-line depreciation.

Step 1. Calculate the sum of the digits of the years of estimated useful life; that is, 4 years $= 1 + 2 + 3 + 4 = 10$.

Step 2. Determine depreciation to be taken in each year, starting in the first year, for the number of years of remaining useful life.

Year of Life	Years Remaining	Rate Fraction		Percent
1	4	$\frac{4}{10}$	$=$	40
2	3	$\frac{3}{10}$	$=$	30
3	2	$\frac{2}{10}$	$=$	20
4	1	$\frac{1}{10}$	$=$	10
10	10			100

Double Declining Balance. The first step in the double-declining-balance method is to determine the rate of depreciation by means of the straight-line method. This figure is then doubled, and then always taken on the declining balance of the value of the asset. The following steps illustrate the double-declining-balance method, again using the machine with a net asset value of $1,000 as an example.

Step 1. Determine rate of depreciation under straight-line method; that is, four years or 25%.

Step 2. Double rate of depreciation used under straight-line method; that is, 25% $\times$ 2 = 50%.

Step 3. Apply rate, always using the declining balance of net asset as the value.

Year	Value	Rate, %	Depreciation	Declining Value
1	$1,000.00	50	$500.00	$500.00
2	500.00	50	250.00	250.00
3	250.00	50	125.00	125.00
4	125.00	50	62.50	62.50
5	62.50	50	31.25	31.25
6	31.25	50	15.62	15.62

• Reserves for Accumulated Depreciation. In accounting, the assets of a business are subject to an invariable life cycle. As they are used to generate revenues for the business, they become an expense. Thus, cash may be used to pay a salesman who is generating revenue through his selling efforts. The asset of cash decreases, and the expense of selling increases. Similarly, when merchandise inventory is sold, the inventory asset decreases, and the expense of cost of goods sold increases.

In accounting for fixed assets, we follow this same approach. Since the fixed asset is consumed in the life of the business, the cost of its usage is taken as an expense called depreciation. The time period involved is longer, and estimates must be made, but the basic procedure, as in all other cases, is to decrease the asset as it is used and increase the expense.

There is one additional difference: The value of the fixed asset on the balance sheet is not reduced directly, as was the case with other forms of assets. Instead, the accountant accumulates these reductions in a special account so that they can be shown separately on the balance sheet. This special account is called a reserve for accumulated depreciation. As depreciation expense is incurred, the accountant increases this cumulative account (sometimes called a "contra account") and at the same time increases the item of depreciation expense that appears in the income statement.

The purpose behind this process is to allow fixed assets to always appear on the balance sheet at their original gross value. The extent to which they have been used can then be determined from the accumulated depreciation account in order to arrive at the estimated net fixed value of the assets. This procedure provides more information to the reader of the financial statement. Fixed assets stay on the balance sheet even though they may be 100 percent depreciated. Thus, it is possible for fixed assets to appear on a balance sheet in the following manner:

Fixed Assets

Gross (property, plant, and equipment)	$283,000
Less reserve for accumulated depreciation	282,000
	$ 1,000

At the time a fixed asset is actually disposed of, the gain or loss on its sale is shown as a nonoperating profit or loss in the income statement. If the fixed asset is sold at an amount greater than originally estimated as its salvage value, there is a gain. If it is sold at an amount less, there is loss.

2. Inventory Accounting. Inventory accounting is concerned with the asset item of inventories and the expense factor of cost-of-goods sold. Earlier, we defined the cost of goods sold as the cost of the product purchased for resale and/or manufactured and ultimately sold to obtain revenue. The cost of goods sold, except in the case of service industries, is by far the largest element of cost in an income statement and is therefore one of the most important items of expense. Since the accountant must always try to match expenses with revenues, only the costs of the goods sold to generate sales revenue will be included in the cost of the goods sold for the period.

• Perpetual Inventory Accounting Procedures. When a business has a limited number of sales, but of a high value—such as yachts—the accountant can easily and practically maintain a record of each individual item in inventory and easily determine the value of inventories and the cost of goods sold. This approach is called "perpetual inventory accounting," and although it's simple, it's practical only for low-volume, high-price businesses where each sale represents a significant part of revenue.

• Deductive Inventory Accounting Procedures. By way of contrast, think of a dime store or supermarket where literally thousands of transactions take place during the day. Perpetual inventory accounting practices are impossible in this situation. The cost of goods sold must be deduced from comparing the amount of goods on hand at the beginning of a period, goods purchased during the period, and goods on hand at the end of the period. The value of the goods purchased during the period can be obtained from records maintained for this purpose. As an illustration, assume the records of a dime store show the following:

Goods on hand, March 31, 1974	$10,000
Purchases during April 1974	13,000
Goods on hand, April 30, 1974	7,000

Thus, we can conclude that the $10,000 of merchandise on hand at the beginning of April, together with the $13,000 purchased during April, left us with total goods available for sale of $23,000 during April. If, at the end of April, $7,000 of goods were on hand, then $16,000 worth of goods must have been sold during that month.

A more conventional, formal accounting presentation of these same facts would appear as follows:

Beginning inventory, April 1, 1974	$10,000
Purchases	13,000
Goods available	$23,000
Less closing inventory	7,000
Cost of goods sold	$16,000

In deducing the cost of goods sold, of course, we are assuming that the merchandise has actually been sold. This may not always be the case, for in fact there may have been shrinkage, spoilage, or even pilferage of the merchandise. The user of accounting data should always bear this possibility in mind.

• Inventory Valuation. Deductive and perpetual inventory accounting procedures provide the accountant with two different methods to use to tally, or register, business inventories and to obtain the cost of goods sold. Additional complexities can be, and often are, associated with the inventory valuation process. Let's take as an example Gerry M.'s brother, the owner of a service station. He, like Gerry, is preparing accounting records for his business. At the end of April he deduced his cost of goods sold in accordance with that date:

Inventories
Regular Motor Gasoline

	No. of Gallons	Price per Gallon	Value
Opening inventory, April 1	10,000	40¢	$4,000
Purchases in April	12,000	40¢	4,800
Goods available	22,000		8,800
Less ending inventory, April 30	8,000		3,200
Cost of goods sold for April	14,000		$5,600

39

There is no problem here. However, in the following month the cost he had to pay for gasoline increased 5 cents a gallon. Data for the month of May appeared as shown below:

Inventories
Regular Motor Gasoline

	No. of Gallons	Price per Gallon	Value
Opening inventory, May 1	8,000	40¢	$3,200
Purchases in May	10,000	45¢	4,500
Goods available	18,000		$7,700
Less inventory, May 31	10,000		
Cost of goods sold for May	8,000		

As a result of the price change, we now have a problem finding the value of the closing inventory. By deduction, we know that during the month of May, Gerry's brother sold 8,000 gallons of gasoline. What we don't know is whether they were bought at the new price of 45 cents a gallon, or at the old price of 40 cents a gallon. The dilemma is placed squarely in the lap of the accountant. He can resolve this particular problem in one of several ways.

First, he can make a so-called FIFO assumption. FIFO, an acronym for "First In, First Out," assumes that goods entering an inventory first are sold first. If in our particular illustration the accountant were to employ the FIFO assumption, the May valuation of inventories and cost of goods sold for Gerry's brother would appear as follows:

Inventories
Regular Motor Gasoline
FIFO APPROACH

	No. of Gallons	Price per Gallon	Value
Opening inventory, May 1	8,000	40¢	$3,200
Purchases in May	10,000	45¢	4,500
Goods available	18,000		$7,700
Less ending inventory, May 31	10,000	45¢	4,500
Cost of goods sold for May	8,000	40¢	$3,200

We can see that under the FIFO assumption, the most current purchases, that is, those made at 45 cents per gallon, are shown as part of the inventory rather than as the cost of goods sold during the accounting period.

A second alternate approach the accountant can employ is LIFO, which stands for "Last In, First Out." The LIFO approach is exactly the opposite of the FIFO approach. It assumes the most recent purchases are the ones that have been sold, so the value of the goods shown in inventory is at the older purchase cost. Here's how the LIFO inventory calculation would change our example:

Inventory
Regular Motor Gasoline
LIFO APPROACH

	No. of Gallons	Price per Gallon	Value
Opening inventory, May 1	8,000	40¢	$3,200
Purchases in May	10,000	45¢	4,500
Goods available	18,000		$7,700
Less ending inventory, May 31	10,000*		4,100
Cost of goods sold for May	8,000	45¢	$3,600

* Made up of 2,000 gallons at 45¢ = $900, and 8,000 gallons at 40¢ = $3,200.

A third alternative is the Average Method, under which the accountant simply averages the costs of the opening inventory and purchases and then the cost of the goods sold for the period at this average. Under this approach we would have the following:

Inventory
Regular Motor Gasoline
AVERAGE METHOD

	No. of Gallons	Price per Gallon	Value
Opening inventory, May 1	8,000	40¢	$3,200
Purchases in May	10,000	45¢	4,500
Goods available	18,000		$7,700
Less ending inventory, May 31	10,000	42.8¢*	4,280
Cost of goods sold for May	8,000		$3,420

* Derived: $7,700 ÷ 18,000 gallons = 42.77¢ per gallon, rounded off to 42.8¢ per gallon.

Obviously, the accountant's choice of method will have an influence on the financial results for the period. A comparison of the gross profit from the sale of regular gasoline for May under the three inventory valuation methods gives these results:

Regular Motor Gasoline
Gross Profit Comparison

	LIFO	FIFO	Average
Sales: 8,000 gallons @ 60¢	$4,800	$4,800	$4,800
Less cost of goods sold	3,600	3,200	3,420
Gross profit	$1,200	$1,600	$1,380
Inventory value to be shown on balance sheet	$4,100	$4,500	$4,280

Under the LIFO approach, the cost of goods sold is higher than it is under either the FIFO or the Average Method. As a consequence, profits will be lower. Clearly, the method chosen can significantly influence the so-called final net book results of the business.

3. Accounts Receivable. This final special accounting problem arises largely because almost all businesses must sell on credit. When they do, they receive an account receivable (a legal obligation to be paid) in lieu of cash. Accounts receivable appear on the balance sheet as an asset. If for some reason the account receivable cannot be collected, it has no value. Fortunately, most accounts receivable are collected; in fact, sound credit practices should prevent a business from selling on credit to anyone from whom it doesn't think it can collect. Despite these precautions, every business ends up with some uncollectable accounts. Various accounting methods are used to deal with them.

The most direct approach is simply to write off a bad debt once it becomes clear that payment will not be received. When this is done, the accountant reduces the value of accounts receivable by the amount of the writeoff and increases the expense; the uncollected payment is called a "bad debt." The problem with this approach is that the accountant has to wait for an actual bad-debt loss to occur before it can be recognized. What is not known is who won't pay and the amounts. To overcome this problem, the general practice is to make a comprehensive estimate of the total amount of accounts receivable that won't be collected. This estimate is called a "reserve for doubtful accounts receivable." The reserve is taken as a reduction from the accounts receivable on the balance sheet and usually appears as shown below:

Accounts receivable	$200,000
Less reserve for doubtful accounts	7,000
	$193,000

While the reserve for doubtful accounts is being created and used to decrease the value of the asset, a corresponding increase occurs in the expense—bad debts. The actual amount to be set up as a reserve for doubtful accounts is usually based on the firm's past experience. Management may determine that a certain percentage of the annual net sales—say, 2 to 3 percent—is appropriate. Alternately, it may make a similar determination on the basis of its credit sales alone, reflecting the reserve in the balance sheet.

On the occasion of an actual bad debt write-off, both the asset of accounts receivable and the reserve are reduced by the amount of the write-off. If we assume a write-off of $1,000, the figures shown above would be modified as follows:

	Before Write-off	After Write-off
Accounts receivable	$200,000	$199,000
Less reserve for doubtful accounts	7,000	6,000
	$193,000	$193,000

As we have seen, accounting for fixed assets, inventory, cost of goods sold, and bad debts involves accounting methods and techniques that are less difficult and enigmatic than they may seem. ∎

Part 3: The basic accounting process

Although the primary purpose of this series is to show how to use rather than how to create accounting data, the nonfinancial manager needs at least an elementary understanding of the basic accounting process. Earlier, we traced the development of Gerry M.'s Furniture Mart by actually changing the balance sheet for the business with each transaction. Although this approach was helpful as background, actually using it to account for an enterprise of any size would be impractical to the point of impossibility.

With a much more practical method, called double-entry accounting, the effects of business transactions are collected in records called "accounts." The simplest form of an account is the so-called T account—which, as the name suggests, looks like this:

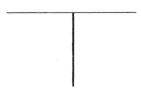

Every item of financial information on the balance sheet and the income statement has an account. There are usually many subaccounts for each item; these are "rolled up" and shown as only one figure on a financial statement. The accountant can create an account for any item of information about the business. For example, he may want to know not only total sales, but sales by such types of customers as government, manufacturers, wholesalers, agents, or retailers. To capture this information, he sets up subaccounts under the general sales account. But no matter how many accounts are set up, they always conform to the general framework of a balance sheet and income statement.

BASIC RULES

The accounting process involves the following basic rules under which accounting information is recorded.

Entry. The recording of a business transaction in an account is referred to as an "accounting entry."

Debits and Credits. An entry on the left-hand side of an account is called a "debit." An entry on the right-hand side is called a "credit."

T Account

Debit	Credit
Entry on left-hand side	Entry on right-hand side

When the terms "debit" and "credit" are used in the accounting process, they have no meaning other than the above. Ignore other connotations of these terms when working with them in accounting.

Balance sheet and income statement accounts increase and decrease with debits and credits in accordance with the following immutable rules:

45

BALANCE SHEET ACCOUNTS

Assets
- Debit entries increase an asset account.
- Credit entries decrease an asset account.

Liabilities
- Debit entries decrease a liability account.
- Credit entries increase a liability account.

Owner's Equity
- Debit entries decrease owner's equity accounts.
- Credit entries increase owner's equity accounts.

INCOME STATEMENT ACCOUNTS

Revenue
- Debit entries decrease revenue accounts.
- Credit entries increase revenue accounts.

Expenses
- Debit entries increase expense accounts.
- Credit entries decrease expense accounts.

Net Income
- Debit entries decrease net income accounts.
- Credit entries increase net income accounts.

These rules are summarized graphically in T account form in Exhibit 4 (page 47), in which the logic of the debit-credit mechanism can be seen. Note, for example, the relationship between the effects of debits and credits in owner's equity accounts and income statement accounts. Owner's equity increases with credits. Revenue, which benefits owner's equity, also increases with credit.

Expenses, as we said sometime earlier, decrease owner's equity. This is shown by debiting the owner's equity account. An increase in expenses is also shown by debiting the expense account.

In previous chapters, we showed that assets decrease as they are consumed, and that through the process of becoming an expense, they reduce owner's equity. Exhibit 4 shows how this would occur through a credit entry to reduce the asset and a debit entry to increase expense (or reduce owner's equity).

Despite the logic of the debit-credit formula, most people (including many practicing accountants) simply commit it to memory rather than think through the logic of every accounting transaction.

Exhibit 4. Double-entry accounting formula.

BALANCE SHEET ACCOUNTS

Assets		Liabilities	
Dr.	**Cr.**	**Dr.**	**Cr.**
+	−	−	+

		Owner's Equity	
		Dr.	**Cr.**
		−	+

INCOME STATEMENT ACCOUNTS

Revenue		Expenses	
Dr.	**Cr.**	**Dr.**	**Cr.**
−	+	+	−

	Net income	
Dr.		**Cr.**
−		+

Key
  + = increase
  − = decrease

A final point here is that all accounting entries must balance. That is, the debits must always equal the credits. Each particular entry may include two or three elements, but they must in the final sum always be equal to the corresponding debit or credit. This is in keeping with the concept of the balance sheet, which requires that assets and equities always be in balance.

FILING SYSTEMS

Two instruments are used to file and record accounting data. One of these is the "accounting ledger," or all the accounts a business uses grouped together. The other is the "accounting journal," a log or document used to record daily events in the language of debits and credits. For example, when a customer appears and pays a bill, the accountant would want to indicate that the business's cash account had increased and that the accounts receivable had decreased. Using the language of debits and credits, he would make an entry in a journal book as follows:

Debit (Dr.) Cash
Credit (Cr.) Accounts receivable

The abbreviated forms—*Dr.* and *Cr.*—are customarily used in making journal entries.

STEPS OF THE ACCOUNTING PROCESS

We can summarize the steps in the accounting process as follows:
1. Analysis of Transactions. The first step in established accounting systems in organizations of some size is to assign an account number to a transaction in keeping with the organization's chart of accounts. A chart of accounts is a list of the various categories of expense and income used to accumulate the results of transactions for management control and for operating statements and balance sheets. Most charts of account use numbering systems that enable the organization to integrate responsibility-reporting systems (in which expenses and, where appropriate, income are associated with a clearly defined organization unit) with financial-reporting systems.

For example, a chart of accounts may use an account number in the form 22.33.444, in which the first two numbers indicate the major organizational unit; the second two numbers, some significant separable activity of that unit, such as a smaller organizational unit, a special project, or a particular product; and the last three numbers, an expense category such as salaries, travel, telephone and telegraph, and so forth.

With these numbers as the basis, income and expenses can be summarized and totaled by major organization unit, by special project, by expense or income category, by reporting categories typically listed on balance sheets and operating statements, or by many possible combinations of these approaches.

Every transaction must be understood and analyzed before it can be accounted for. In this step, the accountant thinks through the effects of the transaction and translates them into specific debits and credits to the appropriate accounts.

2. Journalization. Journalization means the daily recording (in terms of debits and credits to the accounts) of each business transaction.

3. Posting. This involves transferring, or posting, the information recorded in the journal to all the accounts in the ledger.

4. Adjusting. In addition to making entries that result from actual business transactions, the accountant has to adjust the accounting of the business for other factors to present its financial situation accurately. Basically, this involves giving appropriate recognition to reduction in the value of an asset through its use or consumption in the business.

Assume that the annual amount of an insurance premium of $1,200 was paid in advance—creating an asset of prepaid insurance. As each month passes, the asset loses some of its value. On a twelve-month basis, the monthly reduction in value is $100. This fact is reflected in the accounts by means of an "adjusting entry" that shows the reduction in the value of the asset and the increase in expense:

Dr. Insurance expense $100
Cr. Prepaid assets (insurance) $100

Depreciation is another basic entry that must be made in each accounting period to adjust the accounts of the business. Like other entries, adjusting entries are included in the journal. Unlike others, they are triggered only by the mental steps the accountant takes to accurately adjust the accounts of the business.

5. Closing. To understand the closing step, we must understand that there are two types of accounts—temporary and real. Accounts for the income statement are temporary; accounts for the balance sheet are real. This means that at the end of the accounting period, whether a month or a year, the so-called temporary or income statement accounts are actually closed out so that the debit and credit sides are equal—thus making the new opening balance zero. Real accounts, or balance sheet accounts, are never closed. They always have a debit or a credit balance.

The closing process involves the steps used to take every account that appears on the income statement and close it (bring it to zero). The final net income account will then be closed to shareholders' equity account on the balance sheet. Later we'll illustrate the accountant's closing procedures with a step-by-step example.

6. Preparation of Financial Statements. This is the final step in the accounting process. It involves extracting information from accounts in the company's ledger and presenting it in accordance with a standard balance sheet and income statement format.

THE ACCOUNTING PROCESS ILLUSTRATED

Let's turn now to an application of these six steps in the accounting process, again using Gerry M.'s business as the example. In reviewing each transaction, we will start by going through the first three of the six steps required—analysis, journalization, and posting. Once this is done, we will continue to adjust and close the accounts, and then prepare financial statements.

As a first step, we need to confirm the opening balances of our various accounts. To do this, we will look at Gerry M.'s balance sheet (see below).

GERRY M.'s FURNITURE MART
Balance Sheet
December 31, 1974

Assets			Equities		
			Accounts payable	$100	
Cash	$ 300		Total current liabilities		$ 100
Accounts receivable	200		Notes payable		2,000
Inventories	3,600		Owner's equity		
Total current assets		$4,100	Capital stock	$5,000	
Fixed assets		5,000	Retained earnings	2,600	
Prepaid assets		600	Total owner's equity		7,600
Total assets		$9,700	Total equities		$9,700

The underlying ledger in support of this balance sheet appears in Exhibit 5 (page 51), which shows that there is a ledger account for every item on the balance sheet. Moreover, the balances in the ledger accounts correspond to the amounts shown on the balance sheet. Since balance sheet accounts are never closed, they always reflect

Exhibit 5. Basic general ledger for balance sheet accounts.

ASSETS		EQUITIES	
Dr. +	Cr. −	Dr. −	Cr. +
Cash		**Accounts Payable**	
$300			$100
Accounts Receivable		**Notes Payable**	
$200			$2,000
Inventories		**Capital Stock**	
$3,600			$5,000
Fixed Assets		**Retained Earnings**	
$5,000			$2,600
Prepaid Assets			
$600			

a credit or debit balance unless there is nothing of value to be recorded in the account.

Exhibit 6 (page 52) shows the so-called temporary or income statement accounts for the furniture mart. Note that none of these shows a balance, since they are temporary accounts and have a balance of zero from the closing of the last accounting period.

Now to our detailed application of the steps in the accounting process. Each transaction described below has a corresponding entry in Exhibit 7, and Transactions 6 and 7 appear in both Exhibit 7 and Exhibit 8 (pages 53 and 54).

• Transaction 1. Customer pays $100 to the furniture mart, settling an outstanding accounts receivable.

Step 1, analysis of transaction. As a result of this transaction, the company has received $100 in cash. The asset cash increases by this amount, and the asset accounts receivable decreases by the same amount.

Step 2, journalization. The formal accounting treatment of this transaction in the journal would be shown:

Dr. Cash $100
    Cr. Accounts receivable $100

Exhibit 6. Basic general ledger for income statement accounts.

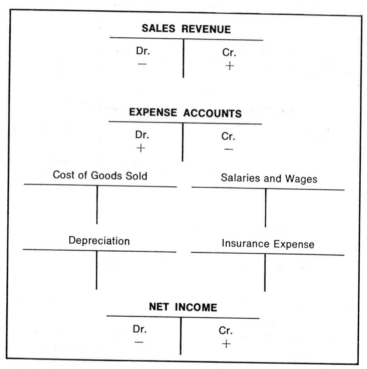

Step 3, posting. The transaction would be posted to the T accounts in the ledger as follows:

Cash

Dr.	Cr.
+	−
$100	

Accounts Receivable

	$100

Exhibit 7. Cumulative postings of balance sheet accounts.

	ASSETS			EQUITIES	
Dr. +		**Cr.** −		**Dr.** −	**Cr.** +

Cash			Accounts Payable		
	$300*				$100*
†(1) $100		$100 (2)		(2) $100	
(3) 5,000		2,000 (4)			
(6) 3,000		1,000 (5)			
		600 (7)			

Accounts Receivable			Notes Payable		
$200*					$2,000*
		$100 (1)		(4) $2,000	

Inventories			Capital Stock		
$3,600*					$5,000*
(5) 1,000		$2,000 (6)			5,000 (3)

Fixed Assets			Retained Earnings		
$5,000*					$2,600*
		$50 adjusting entry			300

Prepaid Assets		
$600*		
		$50 adjusting entry

* Indicates opening balance
† Numbers in parentheses indicate transactions

Exhibit 8. Cumulative postings of income statement accounts.

SALES REVENUE

Dr.	Cr.
—	+
	$3,000 (6)*

EXPENSE ACCOUNTS

Dr.	Cr.
+	—

Cost of Goods Sold		Salaries and Wages	
(6)* $2,000		(7)* $600	

Depreciation		Insurance Expense	
$50†		$50†	

NET INCOME

Dr.	Cr.
—	+

Key
* Numbers in parentheses indicate transactions.
† Adjusting entry.

● Transaction 2. The furniture mart pays $100 to a creditor, settling an account.

Step 1, analysis of transaction. The asset cash has been decreased by $100. At the same time a liability in the amount of $100, which was previously an account payable, has been reduced by the same amount.

Step 2, journalization.

Dr. Accounts payable $100
   Cr. Cash $100

Step 3, posting. The transaction would be posted to the T accounts in the ledger as follows:

Cash		Accounts Payable	
Dr.	Cr.	Dr.	Cr.
+	—	—	+
	$100	$100	

• Transaction 3. The furniture mart issues stock for a value of $5,000 to various members of Gerry M.'s family, receiving cash.

Step 1, analysis of transaction. The company has received $5,000 in cash, and the amount of this asset is increased by $5,000. At the same time, capital stock has been increased, since the sale of stock was the source of these funds. That equity increases by $5,000.

Step 2, journalization.

    Dr. Cash $5,000
        Cr. Capital stock $5,000

Step 3, posting. This transaction would be posted to the T accounts in the ledger as follows:

Cash		Capital Stock	
Dr.	Cr.	Dr.	Cr.
+	—	—	+
$5,000			$5,000

• Transaction 4. The furniture mart uses some of the proceeds it received from its stock issue to pay off its $2,000 note payable.

Step 1, analysis of transaction. The company has reduced its asset cash in the amount of $2,000. At the same time it has reduced a liability to a creditor, or a claim on its assets, by the same $2,000.

Step 2, journalization.

    Dr. Notes payable $2,000
        Cr. Cash $2,000

Step 3, posting. See the Cash Account and the Notes Payable Account in Exhibit 7.

• Transaction 5. The company purchases merchandise for $1,000 in cash.

Step 1, analysis of transaction. The company has increased one of its assets, merchandise. At the same time, it has used another asset to make this purchase, cash, which has to be decreased.

Step 2, journalization.

> *Dr.* Merchandise inventory $1,000
>   *Cr.* Cash $1,000

Step 3, posting. See the Cash Account and Inventories Account in Exhibit 7.

• Transaction 6. The furniture mart sells, for $3,000 cash, merchandise that cost $2,000.

Step 1, analysis of transaction. Several things happen because of this transaction. It is the first event to affect the income statement, since the company has delivered merchandise and thereby obtained increased revenue. At the same time, because the merchandise was sold for cash, this asset is increased. In exchange, the furniture mart turns over merchandise that cost $2,000, decreasing the value of its inventory by this amount. This increases its expense, cost of goods sold, by the same amount.

Step 2, journalization. Journal entries for this transaction, because it involves several accounts, are four:

> *Dr.* Cash (Exhibit 7) $3,000
>   *Cr.* Revenue (Exhibit 8) $3,000
>
> *Dr.* Cost of goods sold (Exhibit 8) $2,000
>   *Cr.* Inventories (Exhibit 7) $2,000

Step 3, posting. This transaction would be posted to the T accounts of the general ledger as follows:

BALANCE SHEET ACCOUNTS (Exhibit 7)		INCOME STATEMENT ACCOUNTS (Exhibit 8)	

Cash

Dr. + $3,000	Cr. —

Revenue

Dr. —	Cr. + $3,000

Inventories

Dr. +	Cr. — $2,000

Cost of Goods Sold

Dr. + $2,000	Cr. —

• Transaction 7. The furniture mart pays $600 of salaries and wages in cash.

Step 1, analysis of transaction. The asset, cash, decreases by $600; the expense, salaries and wages, increases by the same amount.

Step 2, journalization.

Dr. Expenses (salaries and wages; Exhibit 8) $600
    Cr. Cash (Exhibit 7) $600

Step 3, posting. This transaction would be posted to the T accounts of the general ledger as follows:

BALANCE SHEET		**INCOME STATEMENT**	
Cash		Salaries and Wages	
Dr.	Cr.	Dr.	Cr.
+	—	+	—
	$600	$600	

For the preceding seven transactions, we have carried out the first three steps involved in the accounting process—analysis, journalization, and posting. In actual practice, the journal would probably be posted to the company's ledger as a separate step, later in the day or even at the end of the week or the month.

• Adjusting. We noted earlier that at the end of each accounting period it is necessary to think through the adjustments that need to be made to accurately reflect the status of the business. Usually these adjustments involve recognition of expense that arises from the use of an asset during the accounting period under consideration.

In our case, there are fixed assets of $5,000 and prepaid assets of $600. The fixed assets consist of a Volkswagen delivery van for which we shall assume an annual depreciation cost of $600. Prepaid assets consist of a prepaid insurance premium. If we assume, for the sake of simplicity, that the business transactions have spanned the period of a month, the values of both these assets need to be adjusted (with a corresponding expense increase) to reflect their usage during this period. In the case of the Volkswagen, if the annual rate of depreciation is $600, then the monthly rate is $50. The accountant needs to reflect a decrease in the value of fixed assets of this amount and a corresponding increase in expense. We said earlier that instead of entering a direct deduction from the value of fixed assets, the accountant uses a reserve for depreciation. We, however, shall simply make the entry directly to fixed assets. The depreciation adjustment for the month of January 1974 would result in the following journal entries:

> *Dr.* Depreciation expense $50
>   *Cr.* Fixed assets $50

The transaction would be posted to T accounts of the general ledger as follows:

BALANCE SHEET		INCOME STATEMENT	
Fixed Assets		Depreciation Expenses	
Dr.	Cr.	Dr.	Cr.
+	—	+	—
	$50	$50	

The prepaid asset consists of an annual insurance premium that has been paid in advance. Its value also decreases at a rate of $50 per month, with adjusting entries that would appear in journal form as follows:

> *Dr.* Insurance expense $50
>   *Cr.* Prepaid assets (Insurance) $50

Posting to T accounts in the ledger, we have:

BALANCE SHEET		INCOME STATEMENT	
Prepaid Assets		Insurance Expense	
Dr.	Cr.	Dr.	Cr.
+	—	+	—
	$50	$50	

● **The Closing Process.** We said earlier that income statement accounts were temporary accounts that had to be closed at the end of each accounting period. This closing involved taking each account and establishing the debit or credit entry necessary to bring the account to a zero balance. The following step-by-step procedure will more clearly illustrate this logical process.

Closing the revenue account. Exhibit 8 (page 54) is the income statement of the furniture mart, with the entries of the transactions posted to each of the T accounts. The first account is revenue, which has a credit balance of $3,000. If we want this account to equal zero, or close it out, we must debit for $3,000. We want to close the revenue account to the net income account so the other half of the entry would be a credit to net income, thus:

Dr. Revenue $3,000
    Cr. Net income $3,000

Closing the expense accounts. The next step is to close the expense accounts to net income. The first of these is cost of goods sold, which has a debit balance of $2,000. To close it, we must make a credit entry of $2,000. That is, the balancing debit portion of the entry must be made to net income for the same amount, thus:

Dr. Net income $2,000
    Cr. Cost of goods sold $2,000

The next expense account is salaries and wages, which has a debit balance of $600. To be closed, it must also have a credit entry of $600, thus:

Dr. Net income $600
    Cr. Salaries and wages $600

The depreciation and insurance accounts show a balance of $50 each. They would receive exactly the same treatment as the other two expense accounts, with a debit to net income in each instance of $50.

Closing the net income account. All the accounts in the income statement have been closed except for the final one, net income. It, too, must be closed. By adding the debits and credits, we can see that there is a debit balance of $2,700 and a credit balance of $3,000.

To close the account, we must make a debit entry of $300. The other half of the entry is to be a credit to retained earnings. In formal form:

Dr. Net income $300
    Cr. Retained earnings, Exhibit 7..................... $300

Throughout the closing process, and particularly in this last step, we can see the consistent relationship between the mechanics of the accounting process and the basic accounting concepts. The credit to retained earnings in the closing of the net income account is, of course, an increase—which is exactly how we described the function of the income statement in conceptual terms.

GERRY M.'s FURNITURE MART
Balance Sheet
January 31, 1974

Assets			Equities	
Cash	$4,700			
Accounts receivable	100		Accounts payable	0
Inventories	2,600		Notes payable	0
Current assets		$ 7,400	Owner's equity	
Fixed assets	$4,950		Capital stock	$10,000
Prepaid assets	550	5,500	Retained earnings	2,900
Total assets		$12,900	Total equities	$12,900

GERRY M.'s FURNITURE MART
Income Statement
For Period Ending January 31, 1974

Sales revenue		$3,000
Less cost of goods sold		2,000
Gross margin		$1,000
Less		
Salaries and wages	600	
Depreciation expense	50	
Insurance expense	50	
Total expenses		700
Net income		$ 300

• **Preparation of Financial Statements.** The final step in the accounting process is the preparation of financial statements. To do this, we simply take the balances that appear in the ledger of accounts for the balance sheet and income statement and cast them into the conventional format for both these statements. (See Exhibit 7 and Exhibit 8.) Examples are shown at left.

We have worked with only a few very simple business transactions to account for Gerry M.'s efforts. But the principles, procedures, and processes discussed in this chapter and employed in the last several illustrations are exactly those that an accountant would use, no matter how numerous or complex the transactions. ■

Part 4: Manufacturing cost essentials

So far, we have dealt only with the concepts and procedures involved in accounting for business transactions that involve the purchase and resale of merchandise. Obviously, however, it would be unrealistic to ignore any discussion of manufacturing cost accounting. Although manufacturing cost accounting, or "cost accounting," as it is usually called, is a subject worthy of lengthier treatment, we shall discuss only some fundamental concepts that lead to a better understanding of the financial results of a manufacturing enterprise.

MERCHANDISING VERSUS MANUFACTURING

Unlike the merchandiser, who merely purchases and resells a product, the manufacturer makes the product he sells. This involves either conversion or fabrication, which starts with some form of raw material subjected to a manufacturing process requiring either machinery or labor, and probably both. Consider the EZI Manufacturing Company, which manufactures widgets. The firm has determined that it costs $10 to make a widget:

- *Material:* $5 for the cost of the raw material.
- *Labor:* $3 for the cost of the labor for the time involved in making the widget.
- *Factory overhead:* $2 for the general costs—including heat, light, power, janitorial services, and similar expenses—of the factory in which the widget is manufactured.

Accounting for the manufacturing costs of material and labor is usually not difficult. Factory overhead is where the wicket—or, if you will, the widget—gets a bit sticky. To see why this is so, let's look at Exhibit 9, on p. 64 ,which shows the categories of costs with which the accountant must work.

Of the five basic types of costs shown in Exhibit 9, the first three—labor, material, and factory overhead—are unique to the manufacturer. The last two, general and administrative expenses and selling expenses, are common to manufacturers and merchandisers. In manufacturing cost accounting, a problem arises because the difference between expenses that are factory overhead and those that are listed under general and administrative expenses is often fuzzy.

Assume, for example, that EZI manufactures widgets in the same building containing offices for the general manager, the accounting staff, the purchasing department, the engineering control group, and the sales department. One accounting problem is to determine how all the costs associated with this building—taxes, insurance, heat and power, and so on—are to be divided between factory overhead and general and administrative expenses. Since the costs are common to both categories, there are no correct scientific delineations. Once we appreciate the difficulty of precise identification of costs in each category, we can turn to the consequences of this problem.

Exhibit 9. Cost elements and their accounting treatment

Cost Elements	Cost of Merchandiser	Cost of Manufacturer	Clear-Cut Product Costs	Clear-Cut Period Costs	Period and Product Cost	Accounting Treatment
Direct labor		X	X			Product
Direct material		X	X			Product
Factory overhead		X			X	Product
						some division made as to product vs. period
General and administrative expenses	X	X			X	Period
Selling expenses	X	X		X		Period

PERIOD VERSUS PRODUCT EXPENSES

Returning to Exhibit 9, we can see that five general categories of costs have been separated into two broad groups—product expenses and period expenses. Product expenses, as the name suggests, vary with each product made. Direct material is an excellent example. We have said that there is $5 of material in every widget; every time another widget is made, the direct material expenses for the accounting period in which it was made increases $5. Labor is also generally considered to be a product cost. It may not always vary as directly with production as does material cost but, like material costs, it can be directly identified with the manufacture of the product.

Period costs generally can be thought of as overhead costs. They consist, as the exhibit shows, of general and administrative and selling expenses. Period costs occur over a period of time, regardless of the volume of goods produced or sold. For example, property taxes on the factory in which the EZI manufactures widgets obviously do not increase with each additional widget that is manufactured. The same would be true for insurance and selling expenses. The accountant can only assign these indirect costs to a period of time, usually on the basis of when they were incurred.

As Exhibit 9 illustrates, the differentiation between period costs and product costs fades in one area. That area includes many types of expenses not readily identifiable as one or the other. In reality, they are probably a bit of both. In manufacturing accounting, however, the accountant *must* make a delineation—and the manner in which he makes it can have a profound influence on the net income reported for the business.

Let's explore this proposition more specifically, recalling the accounting life cycle of converting assets to expenses. As an asset is consumed in the business, it becomes an expense. When goods are purchased, they become an asset, inventory. At the time of sale, when they are turned over to the customer, they become an expense, cost of goods sold.

The manufacturer also carries inventories—but he makes them instead of purchasing them. The values that he assigns to his inventories and his cost of goods sold are what it has cost him to make the product. The costs to make a manufactured product are those of material, labor, and factory overhead.

As we have seen, however, there is considerable imprecision in differentiating between factory overhead and general and administrative expenses. If the accountant decides that some of the expenses in the area between period costs and product costs are in fact product costs, then these costs are reflected as part of the value of the manufacturer's inventory. Thus, *they are shown as an asset rather than as an expense until the products are sold.* If, conversely, the accountant decides that the expense in question is a period expense, *it is shown as an expense for the accounting period rather than as an asset.*

To illustrate this phenomenon, let's look at XYZ Tool Machinery, Inc., and at the dramatically different financial results the company can obtain from the same manufacturing costs—depending on the decisions it makes regarding period versus product costs. (See the box below.)

XYZ TOOL MACHINERY, INC.
Production for Period: Five Units (Machine Tools)
Sales for Period: Three Units (Machine Tools)

Costs to Produce and Sell Five Units

Labor	$250,000
Material	200,000

Overhead
  Factory
  General and
  administrative
	} 500,000

Selling	100,000

The distinction between factory overhead and general and administrative expenses is unclear. In Case A (see Exhibit 10, page 67), the accountant assumes that 80 percent of overhead costs are product costs. In Case B he assumes that only 50 percent of the overhead costs are product costs. With these assumptions, the calculation of product costs for the cost of goods sold and inventories for the period would be as shown in Exhibit 10. The net income for the period, on the basis of the sales of three units of machine tools at a price of $250,000 per unit, would appear as in Exhibit 11.

We will leave unanswered here the question of whether the company made or lost money. In practice, and with a great deal more information, accountants would arrive at a consensus.

Exhibit 10. Calculation of cost of goods sold and general and administrative expenses

COST OF GOODS SOLD

	Case A		Case B	
	Total	Per Unit	Total	Per Unit
Labor	$250,000	$ 50,000	$250,000	$ 50,000
Materials	200,000	40,000	200,000	40,000
Overhead				
80% × $500,000	400,000	80,000		
50% × $500,000			250,000	50,000
Totals	$850,000	$170,000	$700,000	$140,000

GENERAL AND ADMINISTRATIVE EXPENSES

	Case A	Case B
Overhead Factory General and administrative	$500,000	$500,000
Designated as factory overhead	$400,000	$250,000
Balance, designated as general and administrative expenses for the period	$100,000	$250,000

THREE MANUFACTURING COST SYSTEMS

Basic as they may be, the concepts and issues we have discussed provide sufficient background for a brief, general discussion of three different types of manufacturing cost systems: absorption cost systems, direct cost systems, and standard cost systems.

• Absorption Cost Systems. Another name for absorption costing is "full costing." In this system, all three elements of manufacturing costs—direct labor, direct material, and factory overhead—are absorbed and charged to the product. Thus, all the manufacturing costs

Exhibit 11. Calculation of net income

	Case A		Case B	
	Per Unit	Total	Per Unit	Total
Sales revenue (3 units)	$250,000	$750,000	$250,000	$750,000
Less cost of goods sold (3 units)	170,000	510,000	140,000	420,000
Gross margin	$ 80,000	$240,000	$110,000	$330,000
Selling expense		100,000		100,000
General and administrative expenses		100,000		250,000
Net income/loss before taxes		40,000		(20,000)
Value of inventory shown on balance sheet at end of accounting period (2 units)		$340,000		$280,000

are totally absorbed; they figure as product expense, and none of them is taken as a period cost.

Absorption costing is the most conventional approach to manufacturing cost accounting. The full absorption approach enables us to know that inventory values on the balance sheet include an element of factory overhead that will not be reflected as an expense in the income statement until the product is sold. We have just discussed some of the difficulties and implications of defining factory overhead costs that must be assigned to the product under the absorption costing system.

• Direct Costing Systems. Although absorption cost accounting systems are mandatory for governmental and public financial reporting, the continuing emphasis on the use of accounting data for management purposes has in recent years led to an alternative method of manufacturing cost accounting, called "direct cost accounting." It is almost always used exclusively for internal purposes, and is therefore employed *in addition to* absorption cost accounting.

In direct cost accounting, only elements that can be clearly and directly identified with the manufacture of each product are charged as the cost of that product—usually only direct material and labor. Thus the subtleties and vagaries of allocating overhead between products and periods are totally avoided.

The effect of direct versus absorption cost accounting is illustrated in Exhibit 12, page 70, which shows that under direct costing the elements of manufacturing overhead are charged not to the product, but rather to the period in which they were incurred. When this approach is used, net income for the period more directly corresponds to the sales activity. Advocates of direct costing argue that it is much more accurate to have net income respond to sales. They further argue that the whole process of overhead determination and allocation to products is fuzzy and difficult—clouding rather than clarifying financial results.

• <u>Standard Cost Systems</u>. Like direct costing, the concepts of standard costing grew out of the continuing search for a more effective use of accounting data for managerial purposes. Throughout our discussion of manufacturing costs, we have been thinking in terms of the costs as they were incurred and recorded in the accounting records of a manufacturing enterprise. Such historical cost data tell management only what costs were. The idea behind standard costing is to provide information on what costs *should* be, rather than simply what they were.

Since standard costs are meant to serve as a criterion for efficiency rather than simply to register what has actually happened, they must be well thought out and accurate. More often than not, they are engineered—determined after a thorough and scientific investigation of what costs should be incurred to manufacture a product. In the EZI Company's manufacture of widgets, for example, a standard costing system would be developed in conjunction with engineers who would, after analysis and time and motion studies, determine that a certain amount of money should be spent for raw materials for each product, and a certain amount of overhead should be incurred under efficient, well-managed conditions. Sometimes standard costs are built up on the basis of past experience and cost data rather than predetermined through engineering studies. Once this system is determined, all that is required is to record the total physical number of units manufactured during a given period, and then to apply the standard cost rate to this volume of production.

Under a standard costing system, actual costs incurred are also accounted for and compared against standard costs; the difference is shown as a variance—favorable or unfavorable. If actual costs are

Exhibit 12. Direct versus absorption cost accounting

	Accounting Period 1	Accounting Period 2
Production in units	5	5
Sales in units	3	7
Sales price per unit	$250,000	$250,000
Costs		
Labor		250,000
Material		200,000
Factory overhead*		250,000
General and administrative expenses .		250,000
Selling		100,000

* Factory overhead and general and administrative expenses have been distributed as per Case B in Exhibit 11.

FACTORY OVERHEAD UNIT COST

Period	Total Factory Overhead Cost	Units Produced	Factory Overhead Per Unit
1	$250,000	5	$50,000
2	250,000	5	50,000

Unit Cost	Absorption	Direct
Labor	$ 50,000	$50,000
Material	40,000	40,000
Factory overhead	50,000	0
Totals	$140,000	$90,000

COSTS OF GOODS SOLD

Period	Sales Units	Absorption Costs Per Unit	Absorption Costs For Period	Direct Costs Per Unit	Direct Costs For Period
1	3	$140,000	$ 420,000	$90,000	$270,000
2	7	140,000	980,000	90,000	630,000
Totals	10		$1,400,000		$900,000

Exhibit 12 continued:
Table showing comparative income statement for EZI Company.

	Absorption Costing		Direct Costing	
	Period 1	Period 2	Period 1	Period 2
Sales:				
Units	3	7	3	7
Revenue	$750,000	$1,750,000	$750,000	$1,750,000
Less				
Labor	150,000	350,000	150,000	350,000
Material	120,000	280,000	120,000	280,000
Factory overhead	150,000	350,000	0	0
Cost of goods sold	420,000	980,000	270,000	630,000
Gross margin	$330,000	$ 770,000	$480,000	$1,120,000
Less				
Factory overhead	0	0	250,000	250,000
Selling expenses	100,000	100,000	100,000	100,000
General and administrative expenses	250,000	250,000	250,000	250,000
Total expenses	$350,000	$ 350,000	$600,000	$ 600,000
Net income/(loss)	(20,000)	420,000	(120,000)	520,000
Cumulative net income	$400,000		$400,000	
Ending inventory				
Units	2	0	2	0
Value	$280,000	0	$180,000	0

less than those established in the standard costing system, the variance is favorable; if actual costs are higher, the variance is unfavorable. Exhibit 13, page 72 shows how the net income for XYZ Tool Machinery, Inc., might be recorded under a standard costing system.

By providing a continuing gauge of efficiency, the standard costing system allows management to take action when necessary to correct a problem or inefficiency more quickly. Also, use of the system can often actually facilitate and simplify the accounting process. This is particularly true in the manufacture of high-volume items, where it becomes extremely difficult to record on an actual basis the cost of

Exhibit 13. Income statement of XYZ Tool Machinery, Inc. under a standard costing system.

<u>Sales</u>	$2,500,000
Less	
Cost of goods sold at standard rate	$1,400,000
Variances	200,000
<u>Cost of goods sold</u>	$1,600,000
<u>Gross profit</u>	$ 900,000
Less	
Selling expenses	200,000
General and administrative expenses	500,000
<u>Total expenses</u>	$ 700,000
<u>Net income before taxes</u>	$ 200,000
Variances	
Material variance (higher cost)	$ 100,000
Labor variance (higher cost)	100,000

manufacture for each unit. It is important to recognize, however, that the final net income must always be based on the actual costs incurred and not the standard cost. A standard costing system can involve standards for only direct costs and/or direct plus full costs. In other words, a standard costing system can be a direct standard costing system or a standard absorption costing system. ■

Part 5: Basic financial analysis

To begin, let us assume nothing and ask the basic question: Why financial analysis? The answer is: Financial analysis provides procedures to facilitate the measurement and evaluation of a business firm's progress toward accomplishment of general business objectives—to wit, earning a satisfactory return on investment and maintaining a satisfactory financial position. Let's explore these objectives in greater detail.

GENERAL BUSINESS OBJECTIVES

• <u>Adequate return on investment.</u> When all is said and done, the dollar figure representing the income of an enterprise really tells us very little unless we know how much investment was required to generate this income. Suppose, for example, we are approached by an entrepreneur who says, "I can guarantee you $3,000 a year if you'll make an investment with me." If the proposed investment is $300,000, we are obviously contemplating something less than a bonanza. But if it's only $30,000, the return appears to be more in line with the investment.

In modern management usage, return on investment (ROI) is now used by itself as a management tool. One of the major objectives of financial analysis is to measure the success a business has in obtaining an adequate return on investment.

• <u>Satisfactory financial condition.</u> The second major criterion for success is maintenance of a satisfactory financial condition. This usually involves two aspects—a short-term financial position and an adequate long-term position—or, to describe it differently, adequate liquidity and adequate solvency. *Liquidity* is the ability of a business to meet its short-term financial obligations promptly and satisfactorily. *Solvency* is its ability to meet its longer term financial obligations.

The techniques of financial analysis can logically be broken down into three groups, according to purpose: to measure liquidity, to measure solvency, and to measure corporate profitability and return on invested funds. Ratios are the primary method used for financial analysis. A ratio is simply the mathematical relationship of one number to another. Percentages are the expression of a ratio when the base is 100. Let's look at some specific applications of ratios and percentages for the three purposes mentioned above. We will use the financial data that appear in the balance sheet and income statement of XYZ Tool Machinery, Inc. as shown in Exhibit 14, opposite.

THREE TECHNIQUES OF FINANCIAL ANALYSIS

• <u>Liquidity analysis.</u> Liquidity is the ability of a corporation to meet its current obligations—which it would do with its current assets. These appear as the first major category on the left-hand side of the balance sheet. They are ranked in order of their liquidity, beginning with the item "cash." On the right-hand side of the balance sheet the converse of current assets is "liabilities," which are ordinarily ranked in order of the immediacy of their payment.

Current assets are, by definition, either in the form of cash or will be converted to cash in the course of a year. Current liabilities are those due and payable within a year. Under normal circumstances, a business would use its current assets to pay its current liabilities.

Current ratio. The first ratio, and one of the most common, that

**Exhibit 14. Balance sheet and income statement for
XYZ Tool Machinery, Inc.**

Balance Sheet
($000)
December 31, 1973

	1972	1973		1972	1973
Current assets			*Current liabilities*		
Cash	$ 40	$ 50	Accounts payable	$ 40	$ 50
Accounts receivable	50	60	Accrued wages	20	30
Inventory	70	60	Accrued taxes	30	20
Prepaid expenses	20	20	Total current		
Total current assets	$180	$190	liabilities	$ 90	$100
Fixed assets			*Long-term liabilities*		
Property, plant,			Bonds payable	70	70
and equipment	$150	$183	Total long-term		
Less accumulated			liabilities	$ 70	$ 70
depreciation	70	80			
Net property, plant,			*Shareholders' equity*		
and equipment	80	103	Common stock	60	60
			Retained earnings	50	73
Total fixed assets	$ 80	$103	Total shareholders'		
Other assets	10	10	equity	$110	$133
Total assets	$270	$303	Total equities	$270	$303

Income Statement
For Period Ending 1973

Sales	$400,000
Less cost of goods sold	280,000
Gross profit	$120,000
Less selling expenses	50,000
Less administrative expenses	20,000
Operating income	$ 50,000
Interest expense	4,200
Income before taxes	$ 45,800
Income taxes	22,800
Net income after taxes	$ 23,000

measures the relationship is called the "current ratio." It is obtained
by dividing the current assets of a business by its current liabilities
and would be calculated from the 1973 figures for XYZ Tool Machinery, Inc.'s balance sheet in Exhibit 14 as follows:

$$\frac{\text{Current assets}}{\text{Current liabilities}} = \frac{190,000}{100,000} = 1.9 \text{ current ratio}$$

We can interpret the current ratio of the company as follows: It has $1.90 of current assets to meet $1.00 of debt due as a current liability. In using ratios for financial analysis, each individual situation must be considered. However, as a general rule, a current ratio of 2 to 1 is considered to be quite healthy in American business practices.

Quick ratio. Current assets usually include three basic items—cash, accounts receivable, and inventories. When we evaluate the liquidity of a company on the basis of its current ratio, we assume that the inventory part of total assets is liquid. However, this assumption may not always be realistic. For example, obsolete merchandise may appear as an item of inventory but, in fact, have no value whatsoever. Or inventory may be represented by several large items that would not necessarily become liquid in a short period of time.

For this reason, a second and more stringent evaluation of a company's liquidity can be obtained by the so-called quick ratio, or what is sometimes called the "acid-test" ratio. The quick ratio is computed by taking the "quick" assets of a corporation, which are defined as cash and accounts receivable, and dividing them by the total current liabilities of the corporation. Using the figures from XYZ Tool Machinery's balance sheet, the quick ratio appears as shown below:

Cash	50,000	$\dfrac{110,000}{100,000} = 1.1$ quick ratio
Accounts receivable	60,000	
Quick assets	110,000	
Current liabilities	100,000	

The company has a quick ratio of 1.1 to 1. If the company were really pressed and were not able to quickly sell the merchandise that it holds in inventory, it would still be able to meet all its current obligations out of both its cash and its accounts receivable. As a general rule of thumb, a quick ratio of 1.1 to 1 is usually considered adequate. Although the quick or acid-test ratio subjects the company to a much more rigorous evaluation of its liquidity, the quick assets include the accounts receivable of the business. Therefore, the ratio implicitly assumes that the accounts receivable are readily collectible and in fact have liquidity. Under normal conditions, we would expect this to be the case.

We can, however, specifically evaluate the collectibility of a business's accounts receivable by determining the relationship of receivables to the total annual sales. The receivable data are available from the balance sheet and the annual sales data appear on the income statement.

Average Collection Period. The figures from XYZ Tool Machinery indicate that receivables at year end 1973 of $60,000 are 15 percent of the total annual sales of $400,000 for the company in 1973. Total sales of the company were made over the period of a year, or 365 days. If the accounts receivable represent 15 percent of annual sales in terms of dollars, they also represent 15 percent of the 365 days over which they were made. This percentage equals about 55 days (rounded). This means that, on the average, the company takes 55 days to collect its accounts receivable. On an individual basis, some of these accounts receivable will be collected in a shorter period of time, and others in a longer period of time. As an overall average, however, 55 calendar days pass before an account receivable is collected and becomes cash. This is often referred to as "the average collection period."

The calculation of this period, as shown above, helps evaluate the liquidity of a company's accounts receivable. If the results for XYZ Tool Machinery yielded an average collection period of 180 days, we would, of course, have a different assessment of the speed with which the accounts receivable could be liquidated to obtain cash for the payment of current liabilities.

Determination of what's par in terms of an average collection for a company is somewhat difficult. It will, of course, fluctuate depending upon the credit terms—that is, the amount of time the firm allows its customers to pay their bills.

Inventory-Turnover Ratio. The quick or acid-test ratio recognizes the potential liquidity problems in inventories but does nothing to actually analyze them. It simply ignores them. As a practical matter, the liquidity of a company's inventories can be even more important than the liquidity of receivables. To analyze the liquidity of inventories, the analyst makes use of the "inventory-turnover ratio," which is quite similar to the average collection period. It is calculated by using the cost of goods sold (from the income statement) divided by the average inventory (from data on this item from the balance sheet). The inventory-turnover ratio for XYZ Tool Machinery would be calculated as follows:

$$\frac{\text{Cost of goods sold for 1973}}{\text{Average inventory year end 1972 and 1973}} = \frac{\$280,000}{(70,000 + 60,000)/2}$$

$$= \frac{\$280,000}{65,000} = 4.3$$

By dividing the average inventory into the cost of sales, we obtain a ratio of 4.3. To interpret this ratio, we employ the same logic used in the average collection period. If the cost of sales is the total cost incurred over a period of one year, 1973, and the average of the inventory at the end of 1972 and 1973 is $65,000, this means that the inventory "turned over" 4.3 times during the year. The company sold its inventory approximately one time every 85 days (365 days divided by 4.3). That is to say, its inventory of $65,000 can be converted to $65,000 of either accounts receivable or cash in a period of a little under three months.

By itself, the inventory-turnover ratio indicates how long it takes a company to liquidate its inventories either into accounts receivable or into cash. Also, a business's inventory-turnover ratios can be revealing when they are compared over a period of time. If over this period the inventory-turnover ratio declines, indications are that the company's product is becoming less salable, indicating difficulties for the company. In some situations, a decline in inventory turnover may be simply a reflection of a general economic slowdown with reduced personal consumption.

Many additional ratios can be used to analyze the company's liquidity. The four we've reviewed, however, present the fundamentals. Let's turn next to the analysis of business solvency.

• Solvency. The distinction between liquidity as the ability to maintain a sound financial position over the short term, and solvency as the ability to maintain a sound financial position over a longer term is more than academic, for a company requires more than short-term capital. In the life of every company, there comes a point when it can no longer finance its operations on the basis of current liabilities. When this occurs, it can look either for long-term debt, involving repayment terms of from five to twenty-five years, or for additional shareholders' equity. Shareholders' equity, which in a corporation involves issuing common (or preferred) stock, is almost always permanent capital. Long-term debt, on the other hand, must be repaid and also bears an interest cost which, along with the principal, must be paid by the business. Nevertheless, for the purposes of most financial analyses, long-term debt can be considered relatively permanent capital. The most common form of long-term debt is bonds, which appear as long-term liabilities on the balance sheet, just above shareholders' equity.

The analysis of corporate solvency involves an examination of the adequacy of the permanent sources of capital available to a business. The first and most common ratio used in this evaluation is the so-called debt-equity ratio.

Debt-equity ratio. This ratio measures the proportion of debt and shareholders' equity that a firm has as permanent capital. This is done by adding the long-term debt and the shareholders' equity to arrive at total permanent capital, and then determining the percentage of each in relationship to the total for the debt-equity ratio. For XYZ Tool Machinery, this would appear as shown below:

Long-term debt (liabilities)	$ 70,000
Shareholders' equity	133,000
Total	$203,000

$$\frac{\text{Long-term Debt: } \$70,000}{\text{Long-term debt + shareholders' equity: } \$203,000} = .35$$

The debt-equity ratio of .35 means that 35 cents of every one dollar of permanent capital is long-term debt. Put another way, the shareholders have invested approximately $2 for every $1 of long-term debt. The interpretation of the debt-equity ratio clearly becomes somewhat judgmental. Obviously, though, if the debt-equity ratio indicated that the long-term debtors of the company had invested more money than the shareholders, there might be cause for concern about the adequacy of the permanent capital available for the company.

A very rough rule of thumb in American business is that a company's debt-equity ratio should not exceed .33. That is to say, it is assumed that over the long term a corporation cannot incur more than $1 of long-term debt for every $3 of permanent capital (long-term debt plus shareholders' equity). Many firms, of course, operate outside this capital structure. A firm with a very high debt-equity ratio or a greater proportion of long-term debt is said to be undercapitalized.

Insufficient shareholders' equity, or undercapitalization, can have several adverse consequences. To assure growth a business must make new investments on a continuing basis. But since long-term debt requires repayment, the earnings that can be reinvested are not always sufficient for this purpose. Therefore, a company with insufficient shareholders' equity may have to restrain its growth.

There is a second way to calculate a debt-equity ratio. Our illustration took the relationship of long-term debt to the total of long-term debt and shareholders' equity. An alternate approach is to determine the proportionate relationship between the long-term debt (liabilities) and the equity capital. In the case of XYZ Tool Machinery, this would be $70,000 to $133,000, or a ratio of .53. This method gives a higher debt-equity ratio.

A clear understanding of the approach used to calculate the debt-equity ratio is imperative for the proper analysis and interpretation of the ratio. The conventional yardstick of a .33 ratio is based on the calculation using the sum of long-term debt (liabilities) and share-holders' equity as the denominator. Also, if a company obtains a disproportionate amount of its capital in the form of long-term debt, it may become burdened with excessively large payments associated with the long-term debt. This particular aspect will now be explored by discussing another ratio associated with solvency, the "times-interest-earned ratio."

Times-Interest-Earned Ratio. Long-term debt may be obtained from a private institution or possibly on the bond market. Whatever the source, however, a fixed annual-interest cost is attached to the use of the capital. As a general rule, when a corporation is unable to pay this annual fixed cost, the creditor has a right to demand payment not only of any interest due but also of the principal of the original sum he loaned. For this reason it becomes important for business to be able to meet its fixed annual-interest obligations.

The ratio that attempts to qualify the company's ability to do this is called the "times-interest-earned ratio," which is calculated as follows. First, the operating income of the company is obtained from the income statement. Second, this figure is divided by the annual-interest expense associated with the company's long-term debt to arrive at the times-interest-earned ratio. The annual-interest cost can usually be obtained from the income statement. However, in some cases it may be necessary to separate the interest cost associated with short-term borrowing from that of long-term borrowing. The times-interest-earned ratio for XYZ Tool Machinery would be calculated this way:

$$\frac{\text{Operating income}}{\text{Interest expense on bonds}} = \frac{\$50,000}{\$4,200} = 11.9$$

From the above, we see that last year the operating profits of the company were 11.9 times greater than the annual amount of interest that it would be required to pay on its long-term debt. Therefore, a very significant change in the level of the company's profitability would have to occur before the company's ability to meet its annual-interest payment was seriously jeopardized. If, for example, the times-interest-earned ratio were only 1.2 or 1.5, we might begin to worry about whether the company could meet these fixed payments in case of a sales or economic slump.

• Profitability. A corporation's liquidity and solvency are probably not too significant unless it is profitable—since profitability is, after all, the *sine qua non* of American corporate enterprise. Let's look at some analytical ratios used to evaluate profitability.

Net Profit as a Percentage of Sales. One of the most common ways to express corporate profitability is to take net profit and express it as a percentage of each dollar of sales. In this ratio, annual net income becomes the numerator of the equation, and the total annual net sales becomes the denominator. Net profits as a percentage of sales of XYZ Tool Machinery would be calculated as follows:

$$\frac{\text{Net income after tax}}{\text{Annual sales}} = \frac{\$23,000}{\$400,000} = 5.7$$

This ratio tells us that on every dollar of sales, the company makes a net profit of 5.7 cents.

Gross Margin. Another commonly used measure of profitability is the gross margin as a percentage of sales. Deducting the cost of goods sold from sales gives you the gross margin. The calculation is exactly the same as net income to sales except that gross profit is used as the numerator. The gross margin as a percent of sales for the company would be calculated as shown below:

$$\frac{\text{Gross profit}}{\text{Annual sales}} = \frac{\$120,000}{\$400,000} = 30\%$$

The gross-margin ratio simply indicates how much the company has in terms of cents per sales dollar remaining to cover the selling and administrative expenses of its operation.

It is obvious that the higher either the gross or net profit is as a percentage of sales, the better. Clearly, it is preferable for a company to make a net-income-to-sales ratio of 10 percent on every sales dollar rather than 5 percent. Likewise, a gross margin of 45 percent is better than a gross margin of 35 percent.

Gross-margin and net-income ratios certainly have their place in financial analysis, but they evaluate only profitability. We can't get a proper perspective until we relate the profitability of a venture to the funds that have been invested. For this evaluation, the financial analyst must turn to ratios that measure profits in relation to investment.

• Return on Investment. Whose investment are we talking about? That of the shareholders? Or perhaps all assets used by the company in its operation? Of the following three definitions, any one can be correct, depending on the circumstances:

Return on Shareholders' Investment. "Return on shareholders' investment" is often also called "return on shareholders' equity." It indicates the return that the shareholders enjoy by relating the net income of the business to the total of the investment they originally made in the form of common stock plus the earnings retained in the business. In this ratio, the numerator is the net income for the period; the denominator is the shareholders' equity. The shareholders' equity can be calculated (1) on the basis of shareholders' equity at the end of the accounting period and (2) on the basis of the average at the beginning and the end of the accounting period.

Using the first approach, we would calculate the return on shareholders' investment for XYZ Tool Machinery as follows:

$$\frac{\text{Net income}}{\text{Shareholders' equity at December 31, 1973}} = \frac{\$23,000}{\$133,000} = 17\%$$

The return on the shareholders' investment in the company is 17 percent. Using the second approach, it would be almost 19 percent.

Compare these returns with the return of 5 to 8 percent they could obtain in a savings account. Little risk is involved in investment in a savings account, whereas some risk is undoubtedly involved in the investment in common stock (witness the dramatic downturn in corporate profits in the recession of 1970). As a general rule, return correlates with risk; thus, the higher the risk, the greater the return.

Although it is useful to think of return in the same context as interests paid on a deposit, we should stress the fact that the amount of cash the shareholder will receive from his investment depends on the dividends paid by the company. It is conceivable that those dividends amount to 100 percent of the earnings. (The ratio that measures the cash the shareholder receives is the dividend-yield ratio.) However, this is not likely to happen, since almost all businesses reinvest some portion of their earnings back into the business to assure continued growth.

Return on Total Capital. The second method for determining return on investment is to consider the investment as the total permanent capital of the corporation, including long-term debt as well as shareholders' equity. Under this formula, all sources of permanent capital are included in the investment. The return on total capital for XYZ Tool Machinery would be calculated as shown in Exhibit 15, below.

Exhibit 15. Return on total investment for XYZ Tool Machinery.

Net income after tax		$ 23,000
Correction for deduction of interest on long-term debt:		
Interest before tax:	$4,200	
Less tax @ 50%	2,100	
Add back to income		2,100
Net income after tax, adjusted for interest expense		$ 25,100
Total capital		
Long-term debt		$ 70,000
Shareholders' equity		133,000
		$203,000

$$\frac{\text{Net income after tax (adjusted for interest)}}{\text{Total capital}} = \frac{\$25,100}{\$203,000} = 12.3\%$$

We can see from that illustration that the net income figure used in the ratio can be adjusted for the effect of interest expense on that income. Because long-term debt is used as part of the investment denominator in this calculation, the expenses associated with this source of capital are added back to net income so as to avoid a distortion.

The return on total capital for the company is less than the return on the shareholders' investment. This is always the case, since the incorporation of long-term debt increases the denominator in a much greater proportion than the increase to the profit numerator as a result of the interest adjustment. When return on investment is calculated with total capital as the investment denominator, the resulting figure obviously no longer reflects the return to shareholders. Rather, it represents the return on the total permanent capital of the corporation, regardless of its source. If this approach is used, a more meaningful evaluation of the profitability of the business can be made.

Assume, for example, that a competitor similar in size and profitability to XYZ Tool Machinery also has a total capital investment of $203,000. However, $100,000 of this amount is in the form of long-term debt, and $103,000 is stockholders' equity. The comparative returns of the two companies are shown in Exhibit 16, opposite.

We can see that the return on shareholders' investment is influenced by the makeup of the business's permanent capital. As Exhibit 16 suggests, an evaluation of return made exclusively on the basis of shareholders' investment can be misleading. For this reason, many analysts believe that return on total capital is a more accurate indication of the adequacy of management's efforts to obtain an adequate return on investment.

Return on Total Assets. Under this approach, the investment denominator is defined as the total assets used by the company to generate its net income, or, to put it another way, the total of all items on the left-hand side of the balance sheet. The calculation for return on total assets for XYZ Tool Machinery would be as follows:

Net income after taxes	$23,000
Add back annual interest expense adjusted for taxes	2,100
Net income adjusted for interest after taxes	$25,100

$$\frac{\$25,100 \text{ (adjusted net income)}}{\$303,000 \text{ (total assets)}} = 8.3\% \text{ return on total assets}$$

In the calculation of return on total assets, all interest expense on both short- and long-term borrowings are added back to the income on an after-tax basis. The rationale for this adjustment is the same as for the return on total capital. When calculated on the basis of total assets, the return for the company is even lower. Here again, the reason is that the investment base has been increased in relation to the profit numerator.

Proponents of the total-asset approach to evaluation of ROI argue that the distinction between permanent and short-term capital is

Exhibit 16. Comparative returns on capital.

	XYZ Tool Machinery	Competitor
Long-term debt	$ 70,000	$100,000
Shareholders' equity	133,000	103,000
Total capital	$203,000	$203,000
Net income	$ 23,000	$ 22,100
Annual interest expense	4,200	6,000
Annual interest expense adjusted for taxes at 50%	2,100	3,000

Calculation of Return on Shareholders' Investment

$$\frac{\text{Reported net income}}{\text{Shareholders' equity}} = \frac{\$\ 23,000}{\$133,000} \text{ or } \frac{\$\ 22,100}{\$103,000}$$

Percent return on shareholders' equity	17%	21%

Calculation of Return on Total Capital

Reported net income	$ 23,000	$ 22,100
Add back annual interest expense adjusted for taxes	2,100	3,000
Totals	$ 25,100	$ 25,100

$$\frac{\text{Reported net income adjusted for interest expense}}{\text{Total capital}} = \frac{\$\ 25,100}{\$203,000} \text{ or } \frac{\$\ 25,100}{\$203,000}$$

Percent return on total capital	12%	12%

fuzzy. They contend that many corporations obtain short-term borrowings and renew them year after year, so that in reality they are *de facto* forms of permanent capital and that the return can be favorably influenced because such capital is excluded from the investment base. Therefore, they argue that the best way to measure managerial performance is to ignore completely the sources of invested funds and instead to study only the results obtained on the total of all funds invested in the business. The return on total assets, of course, accomplishes this objective.

Each particular approach to evaluating return on investment has its relevance, depending on the purpose of the analysis. There is not necessarily one best way. Above all, the nonfinancial executive should appreciate the fact that there are several approaches to evaluating return on investment. The results and, more important, the conclusions drawn, can vary with the method employed.

Further ROI Analyses. Return on investment is actually a composite of many factors (Exhibit 17, below). Although return on investment is expressed as a single result, it is actually dependent upon the interplay of important factors. The first factor is the rate at which the business's investment is turned over. Generally speaking, adequate turnover—the rate at which the assets are used to generate sales revenue—comes from successful sales efforts.

Exhibit 17. Components of return on investment.

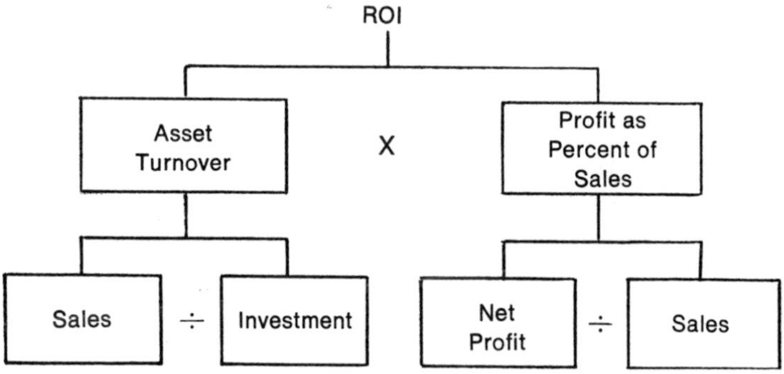

The second factor that influences return on investment is the percentage relationship of net income to each dollar of sales (by itself an analytical ratio that we reviewed earlier). The net-income-to-sales ratio generally depends on the ability of the company to control its costs. Businesses use different combinations of the profit and turnover elements to generate a return on invested funds. In fact, there is an old saying, "Are you in business for fast pennies or slow nickels?" The following table illustrates this particular statement.

	Company A Fast Pennies	Company B Slow Nickels
Sales	$5,000,000	$5,000,000
Net income	50,000	250,000
Investment	500,000	2,500,000
Net income as % sales	1%	5%
Investment turnover	10	2
ROI	1% × 10 = 10%	2% × 5 = 10%

The reader will readily recognize various types of businesses that fit into the two general categories. The local supermarket and dime store are probably classic illustrations of businesses that earn their return in terms of fast pennies; that is, they have a relatively low net income as a percentage of sales, but they turn over their assets many times during the year to generate their return. A marina selling yachts is a good example of the so-called slow-nickels approach to generate a return. This type of business has a much higher profit on each dollar of sales but turns over assets much less frequently.

What might be called the component method of analyzing return on investment was first used by the Du Pont Company as an integral part of its management-control system and has now gained wide acceptance and use in other companies as a management tool.

FINANCIAL ANALYSIS: SOME DISCLAIMERS

The techniques of financial analysis can be extremely effective instruments for incisive and meaningful interpretations of accounting data. They should always be used, however, with full appreciation of the limitations of the particular accounting data from which they are generated. These have been touched upon at various points in this book, and are included in the considerations below.

• Money Only. Accounting measures business results only in terms of money. With this constraint significant aspects of a business may be overlooked—both in the accounting records and in a financial analysis of them.

• History. The past may be prologue, but the chances of this being true in today's dynamic and changing business world are remote. Accounting data are historical. They track only where a business has been. Ratios derived from this history beg the really difficult question of where a business is going.

• The Cost Concept. Under the cost concept, most balance sheet values are at cost. Despite its advantages, this particular approach has limitations that grow even more pronounced as the rate of inflation in the United States increases. Accounting data based on the cost concept are in a certain sense unrealistic. The ratios developed from this data suffer the same deficiency.

• Options. Accounting is much more an art than a science—at least in the sense that much is left to the discretion of the accountant. There are options, however, such as the choice of LIFO, FIFO, or the Average Method; in methods of depreciation; in estimates of the salvage value of fixed assets; and in manufacturing cost methods.

Financial ratios, like all other management tools, are an aid to—but not a substitute for—sound business judgment. ■